TAKING YOUR OWN CASE TO COURT OR TRIBUNAL

a Consumer Publication

Consumers' Association
publishers of **Which?**
14 Buckingham Street
London WC2N 6DS

AD 08594

50p

344

12 FEB 1986

a Consumer Publication

edited by   Edith Rudinger

published by   Consumers' Association
                     publishers of **Which?**

illustrations by   Jo Bampton

© Consumers' Association   September 1985

ISBN 0 340 37255 9
     0 85202 303 0

photoset by Paston Press, Norwich
printed in Great Britain by Page Bros (Norwich) Ltd

contents

Throughout this book

for 'he' read 'he or she'

before starting a case

The first thing you should ask yourself is: am I capable of handling this on my own? It is important to be confident, but also to recognise your own limitations. It would be madness to try and take on a particularly complicated legal action without legal help. Not using a lawyer would save you money initially but that could be a false economy, particularly if your case goes to the High Court, where your opponent will almost certainly have a solicitor and a barrister.

It is essential

- to be clear about the facts on which your case depends
- to have some guidance about the law that is involved
- to know that you can produce sufficient evidence to prove the case
- to ensure as far as possible that your opponent is worth suing – so that if you are successful, he will be able to pay.

There would be little satisfaction in suing successfully where the chances of recovering your loss are minimal. What is more, you will incur the expense of paying court fees, and spend time fruitlessly on preparing and presenting your case.

You must be clear as to what you want to achieve and what your claim is for. Concentrate on that and do not let yourself be distracted by anger or self-righteousness. Above all, do not start an action if your only motive is revenge.

preliminary advice

It is advisable to get some informed advice before starting proceedings. Advice can usually be obtained from a consumer advice centre in appropriate cases, and from citizens advice bureaux.

A citizens advice bureau (CAB) will not only advise you on the strength (or weakness) of your case, but will help you with the various steps if you decide to proceed. Nearly half the CABx have a volunteer solicitor (a few employ a full-time solicitor) who will give advice free. A CAB is usually the best source of information about other specialist advice agencies in an area, and will have relevant leaflets and documents about particular situations.

Where the dispute is to do with rights and obligations under a tenancy, find out if there is a housing advice or aid centre run by the local authority or by a voluntary body in your area who can advise you.

When you go to any advice agency, make sure that you have the relevant papers and facts with you.

legal advice

In some parts of the country there are free legal advice centres, staffed by volunteer lawyers. The centres usually cannot offer further assistance with representation. Some universities and polytechnics operate a legal advice service which is open to members of the public.

There are also a number of law centres with full-time legal staff who will give preliminary advice, and can handle a case from beginning to end, including representation at court or tribunal. There is no charge for the service, but a centre is unlikely to take up a case for someone who can afford to pay solicitors' fees. A law centre only deals with people living, or working, in its area. The Law Centres Federation (Duchess House, 13-18 Warren Street, London W1P 5DB) can give further information about the whereabouts and scope of law centres.

Legal advice agencies which are staffed by qualified lawyers are listed in a *Directory of Legal Advice and Law Centres*, issued by the Legal Action Group (1984 edition £2 from LAG, 242-244 Pentonville Road, London N1 9UN) which should be available at a local library. The Directory includes information about tribunal assistance schemes to which you may be referred by another agency.

Many solicitors will give up to half-an-hour's advice for a fixed fee of £5. Ask the firm of solicitors that you want to go to whether they do so. This is generally money well spent, provided you have prepared your facts and questions beforehand and take all the relevant documents with you so that you do not waste the allotted time.

You can usefully consult a solicitor at the start of a case and then, with that good base, carry on yourself.

the 'green form' legal advice scheme

You may be entitled to some free or reasonably cheap legal advice under the 'green form' scheme administered by the Law Society. The scheme entitles you to up to £50-worth of legal advice – this amounts to about two hours' work or one hour's interview and up to about 10 letters or telephone calls, but cannot include representation in a county court.

Eligibility for the green form scheme is based on financial limits, not the merits of your case. The solicitor will have to ask about your savings and other capital and about your gross weekly income, your outgoings and any dependants, to find out whether your 'disposable capital' and 'disposable income' are within the relatively low limits of the scheme.

Anyone receiving supplementary benefit or family income supplement is automatically eligible for the green form scheme, unless the disposable capital is above the limit.

The solicitor will tell you straightaway if you are eligible. If your disposable income is between £51 and £108 a week, a contribution will be required from you. This is a single payment of between £5 and £60 on a scale based on your income. It has to be paid straightaway (but you may be allowed to pay in instalments).

It is probably worthwhile to get advice under the green form scheme even if you have to pay a contribution. The cost of legal advice will undoubtedly be more if you pay a solicitor privately, and under the green form scheme you will be exempt from court fees.

If you get help under the green form scheme, win your case and get a money settlement, you could be liable for the legal aid fund's 'statutory charge' – that is, you have to pay back the solicitor's costs out of the proceeds.

Which? help

The Which? Personal Service (available on annual subscription from Consumers' Association, 14 Buckingham Street, London WC2N 6DS) has been set up to help its members when they have problems with the goods or services they buy. Its team of lawyers give members active help throughout the stages of their problem by drafting letters, giving advice and, where necessary, preparing the documents to enable them to take their case to court. The notes prepared by the Which? Personal Service give additional help to members when dealing with the situations they will meet in pursuing a claim under the small claims procedure in the county court.

your side of the story

Once you have decided to go ahead, you should concentrate on how you will put your case across when it comes to a hearing.

Bear in mind that the judge, registrar, magistrates, tribunal members will, in effect, hear two stories, which usually conflict, and that a decision will have to be made on the merits of those stories. It is essential, therefore, that your story be presented in the most credible and understandable way and you should look upon your evidence and that of your witnesses in that light. Regard the whole exercise as having to convince the listener that what you are saying is correct.

You must understand what law is involved: without that understanding, there is no point in your proceeding with the case. The legal section in your local reference library may have some relevant books. It may be worth spending £5 to £20 on a brief consultation with a solicitor to check on legal points and on the relevant sections of any Act that is involved or any case that is relevant. Before you go to the solicitor, make sure that you know what you want to ask so that your interview can be kept as short – and therefore as inexpensive – as possible.

Wherever your case is to be – in the county court or the magistrates' court, or before a tribunal – you should, if you can, spend a morning there watching and listening to other cases. This will give you the feel of the hearing and also give you some indication as to what happens when and who should be making it happen.

At the hearing itself, one of the most important pieces of advice is to keep the presentation of your case as simple as possible. Since you are not experienced in court or tribunal procedure, nor in the law, do not complicate matters unnecessarily. Concentrate on putting the facts forward properly, so that the court or tribunal understands what the case is about. In the main, success depends on your being able to get your story across, rather than attempting some dramatic destruction of the other side in cross-examination.

You are the only one who really knows your side of the story; therein lies your strength.

the county court

The majority of civil disputes in England and Wales (there are some differences in Northern Ireland and a different system operates in Scotland) are dealt with by a county court or the High Court. Appeals from those courts go to the Court of Appeal and even up to the House of Lords.

The county court system was established in 1846 to provide local courts to deal with relatively minor cases. The jurisdiction of the county court includes

• general claims for payment of money where the sum involved – whether by way of debt or compensation – is £5,000 or less
• the majority of actions for possession of flats and houses where the rateable value of the property is not over £750 (£1,500 in London)
• claims affecting matrimonial property, maintenance, domestic violence, custody; undefended divorces.

Actions in the county court are heard either by a circuit judge or by a registrar. The circuit judge spends a substantial amount of his time hearing criminal cases and only part of his time in the county court. The registrar is a judicial officer appointed full-time to a county court or a group of county courts. In addition to judge and registrar, each court is staffed by court servants under the direction of a chief clerk, and there is a staff of bailiffs who are responsible mainly for the enforcement of judgments of the court.

In county court procedure, some effort is made to provide for the needs of 'litigants in person' – that is, individuals appearing in court without legal representation. Generally, the judge or registrar hearing the case will help an unrepresented litigant wherever practicable.

Many litigants in person successfully conduct their own case in the county court. Much depends on an ability to frame relevant questions to probe one's opponent's evidence and being able to present the relevant evidence that is needed to prove one's own case.

There is a free booklet issued by the Lord Chancellor's Department and available at county courts, *Small claims in the county court*, on how to sue and defend actions without a solicitor.

small claims

In 1971, in an effort to enable small claims to be dealt with by the courts in cases where the amount involved would make it uneconomic to employ solicitors, the then Lord Chancellor initiated the 'small claims' or 'arbitration' system.

There is, in fact, no separate 'small claims court' but the rules provide for a simplified procedure to be followed in the county court. This applies automatically in all cases where only money is being claimed and the amount is £500 (£300 in Northern Ireland) or less and the case is defended. There is a right to apply to have the action heard in open court but on a limited number of grounds – for instance, alleged fraud, or where the action involves complex matters of fact and law.

In addition to actions for £500 or less, the small claims or arbitration procedure can be used in any case within the normal county court limits where both parties agree or where one party applies for arbitration and the registrar considers the case suitable for arbitration. Many arbitrations do take place where the sum involved is substantially more than £500.

The advantages of this arbitration procedure are that it tends to be swifter and less formal; the normal rules of court procedure do not apply nor do the rules as to evidence necessarily apply; the costs in cases where the amount claimed is £500 or less are generally limited to out-of-pocket expenses (the only solicitors' charges recoverable being the 'costs for issuing the summons' which would amount to about £35). An exception to the rule disallowing costs is that costs can be awarded if the registrar certifies that they have been incurred by the unreasonable conduct of the other party. Also, costs can be awarded in the usual way where there is an arbitration on a claim exceeding £500 (whether or not the eventual amount awarded to the successful plaintiff is less than £500).

Generally, the decision of the registrar or other arbitrator is binding and there is no general right of appeal. There is a limited right to apply to the judge to set aside the arbitration award where there is misconduct or an error of law on the part of the arbitrator.

first steps

It is only worth pursuing a case if you can be reasonably certain that the facts will show that the other person was liable for your loss and if the loss can be compensated by money. You also have to decide how much money to claim. This can include the cost of remedying any breach of contract (for example, of putting right bad workmanship) and the cost of repairing damage caused by the defendant's negligence. It can also include compensation for personal injury and for inconvenience or distress caused by the actions of the defendant.

A crucial aspect is whether the other side will be able to pay. It is difficult to obtain information about another person's financial position. You could perhaps try to find out what sort of accommodation he has; you may be able to discover whether he is working. It is possible to make a search in the index of attachment of earnings orders in the county court for the area in which the proposed defendant lives and to make a search in the register of county court judgments at 99-101 Redcross Way, London SE1 1EE (the fee is £1 if you go in person; for a postal search, minimum fee £2). Such searches will reveal whether there is a court order against your proposed defendant on which he has not paid up. This does not necessarily mean that he (or she) is not worth suing, but would be some warning.

Having satisfied yourself that you have a reasonable claim and that there is no obvious reason why the other person or firm should not be able to pay up, the next step is to write to the proposed defendant saying that unless he settles your claim (pays up or does what you have been asking) within, say, 7 days, you will start court proceedings. This is a sensible and courteous step and failure to take it could mean that you would not be able to recover the court fee from the other party if you should win the case. Send the letter by recorded delivery and keep a copy of it – and of all subsequent ones.

Assuming that the defendant does not pay up or still does not do what is asked of him, the next step is to issue a summons in the county court. The procedure is the same whether the action is to be heard by arbitration or in open court.

which court?
There is a county court in most towns of any size (address under 'courts' in the telephone directory).

The appropriate court is in most cases either the court for the area in which the defendant lives or carries on business, or for the area in which the cause of action arose. Thus, if you live in Reading and were involved in an accident in Putney with a car driven by someone who lives at Southend, you could start with proceedings in the Wandsworth county court (in whose area Putney is situated) or in the Southend-on-Sea county court – but not in the Reading county court. When suing on a debt, the cause of action usually arises where the plaintiff lives or carries on business, because that is where the payment is to take place (unless otherwise agreed).

If you start proceedings in the wrong court, this does not invalidate them. The registrar of that court can decide whether to keep the proceedings there or transfer them to the correct court.

Your local county court will be able to tell you in which court's area the defendant's address is or the place where the cause of action arose is and give you those courts' addresses. They can let you have the necesssary forms for use in another court.

the summons

In order to issue a summons, you need to get from the county court office

* a request for issue of summons
* two copies of the form for your particulars of claim (plus one for any additional defendant).

County court staff know the procedure and will help you fill in these forms, and further ones later. Do not be afraid to ask. They will let you have any of the prescribed 'N' forms you may need. But they should not be expected to give legal advice, and are not qualified to do so.

which kind of summons?

A county court action begins with either a default summons or a fixed-date summons being issued by the court at the request of the plaintiff – the person who brings the action.

A default summons is used for all money claims, whether or not the precise sum is known – for example, when a shop is suing for an unpaid bill or a person is seeking to recover the sum of money he lent to another. Where a person does not know the exact amount from the start

– for example, claiming compensation for being injured in a road accident – the case is also begun by a default summons.

No date for a hearing is fixed when a default summons is issued, and if the defendant fails to file a defence (that is, send to the court office the appropriate document) within the prescribed time, the plaintiff is entitled to have judgment in his favour without a hearing, by default – hence the name default summons.

A fixed-date summons (so-called because a date for a hearing is fixed there and then) is appropriate if the claim is for something other than money – for example, possession of property or delivery of goods.

Certain cases – primarily claims for custody of children under the Guardianship of Minors Act, claims for matrimonial injunctions – are begun not by a summons but by what is called an originating application. At the time of the application, the date is fixed for a hearing. Failure to file a defence does not, of itself, entitle the plaintiff to obtain judgment: he must attend on the hearing date and be prepared to prove his case.

The form of request for a default summons is form N.201; for a fixed-date summons, form N.203 (or N.204 for a summons for recovery of land). They are fairly straightforward forms. One completed copy has to be lodged with the court, and it is sensible to keep a copy for yourself. If you do not want to ask for a case involving over £500 to be referred to arbitration, you should strike out the request for this at the end of the form.

If you are suing a limited company, you must state the registered office of that company: no other address will do. The registered office should be shown on the letters or invoices from the company; if not, you will have to make a search at the Companies Registration Office (Companies House, Crown Way, Maindy, Cardiff CF4 3UZ). This can be done by post for a fee of £2.40 for a photocopy of the entry in the register. There is no fee for a personal search, which can also be made at 55-71 City Road, London EC1. For a company registered in Scotland, the Registrar of Companies is at 102 George Street, Edinburgh EH2 3DJ and the search fee is £1 in person, £2 by post.

particulars of claim

The county court can provide standard forms on which to give the particulars of claim for

* request for return of goods
* claim for cost of goods supplied or services rendered
* claim relating to defective goods
* road accident claim
* possession of rented property.

Get three copies – two to take to the court and one for yourself (otherwise you will have to take photocopies).

If a standard form of particulars of claim applies to your case, you should have no difficulty in completing it. Make sure that you include all relevant facts on which you are relying. Do not at this stage supply any witnesses' statements.

If none of the standard forms covers your case, you will have to prepare your own particulars. You may want to get legal help for this.

The particulars of claim – as all documents lodged with the court – must be headed with the name of the court, a space for the number of the case, and full names of the parties (if known) and then a description of the document:

IN THE ANYTOWN COUNTY COURT

Case No. . . .

(this will be completed by the court office)

BETWEEN

JOHN WILLIAM BLOGGS   plaintiff

and

RAYMOND BROWN   defendant

PARTICULARS OF CLAIM

You should then go on to set out in numbered paragraphs the facts on which you rely. For example, if your neighbour has removed your fence, the particulars of claim might state:

1. The plaintiff is the owner of 13 Acacia Avenue, Anytown.
2. The defendant is the owner or tenant of 11 Acacia Avenue, Anytown.
3. The fence between 11 and 13 Acacia Avenue, Anytown, is erected on land forming part of 13 Acacia Avenue and is the property of the owner of 13 Acacia Avenue.
4. On the 1st January 1985 at about 1.30 a.m. the defendant took down and removed the fence.
5. The cost of replacing the fence is £350 and the plaintiff claims:
   (a) damages limited to £500
   (b) interest
   (c) costs.

The particulars of claim must be dated and signed by the plaintiff who has to give his address for service – that is, where subsequent documents are to be sent.

Dated this . . . . day of . . . . 1985.

Signed: J. W. BLOGGS
whose address for service is
13 Acacia Avenue, Anytown.

5(a) damages
Damages consist of compensation – that is, paying you back for expenses or losses you have incurred, or compensating you for loss, injury or damage you have sustained. Damages are either 'special' or 'general'.

Special damages consist of precise amounts already calculated, items which you have incurred as expenditure or a loss which you can pinpoint in amount. A sum is special damages even if it is only an estimate, in the sense that the actual amount will be a precise sum but is not yet exactly known, so an estimated figure is put in.

In the case of general damages, there is no precise known amount that is being claimed. Instead, the general loss or damage suffered will be compensated by a round sum, to be awarded by the judge. Examples are compensation for injury to the back or loss of a finger.

Details of special damages have to be given: for example,

cost of repairing car	£150
cost of damaged clothing	20
cost of alternative transport	40
	£210

General damages are claimed by saying, for example,

"and the plaintiff claims damages for inconvenience, loss of use of the car, personal injuries etc, limited to £ . . . ."

You have to pay a court fee when you start a county court case, and you pay according to the amount you are claiming. If you do not put in a sum as the top limit of the amount claimed, you have to pay a fee to cover the maximum amount you could theoretically get.

In the case of the Acacia Avenue fence, Mr John Bloggs could have put in at point 5(a) "damages limited to £350". But quite often there are additional or increased costs by the time the action comes to court. Since there is no difference in court fees between a claim for £350 and £500, it was sensible for Mr Bloggs to claim the higher amount.

If expenses are continuing up to the date of trial – for example, in an injury case, fares to hospital – you should put "Fares to hospital 10 times @ £3 (and continuing)" otherwise you will not be able to claim for amounts incurred between particulars of claim and trial.

5(b) interest

You can ask for interest on the amount of special damages that you are claiming from the date that that sum became due to you – for example, when you paid out money or money should have been paid to you – up to the date of the judgment.

The rate of interest that can be claimed is fixed by law (at present, it is 15%) unless there is an agreement between you and the defendant under which interest is payable at a higher rate. If, for example, you are claiming repayment of a loan of £400 on which the defendant had agreed to pay interest at 17%, you would be entitled to claim interest at that rate.

Calculate the amount of interest up to the date that you issue the summons and then work out the daily rate so that any further sums can be calculated up to the date of the judgment. (This can be done with a simple calculator.)

A claim for interest would read as follows:

* interest pursuant to s. 69 of the County Courts Act 1984 at 15% amounting to £xx to the date of this claim and £yy per day thereafter until judgment is given.

  or

* interest as agreed between the plaintiff and the defendant at 17% amounting to £xx to the date of this claim and £yy per day thereafter until judgment is given.

court fees

The request for the summons can be taken in person or sent by post to the court office, together with the two copies of particulars of claim and the fee, which can be paid by cheque, postal order or cash.

The court will tell you the amount of the court fee. At present, court fees are:

amount claimed	court fee
not exceeding £300	10p for every £1 (or part thereof); minimum fee £6
over £300 up to £500	£35
over £500, or no particular amount specified	£40

what the court does next

The court office checks the documents and a number is assigned to the case. The number starts with the last two digits of the year, followed by a five figure reference number, for example, 85.00166. This number is the only way in which the court office can trace the papers relating to your case so it is vital that all letters and communications to the court quote the case number. It is sensible also always to refer to the title of the case, which consists of the surnames of the plaintiff and the defendant: *Bloggs v Brown 85.00166* (*v = versus =* against).

The court office then prepares a summons which is posted ('served') by the court to the defendant, together with a copy of the particulars of claim.

The plaintiff receives from the court office a 'plaint note' which gives the title and number of the case and also the date of service. Keep the plaint note, you will need it later.

date of service

Except where you are suing a limited company, the date of service is deemed to have been 7 days after the date on which the court posts the summons to the defendant. It is an assumed date, not the actual date on which the defendant receives the summons.

This rule applies to postal service. If the summons is served personally by handing a copy to the defendant, then the date when this is done is the 'date of service'. Nowadays, however, nearly all summonses are served by post.

Where the defendant is a limited company, service is deemed to be on the day on which a letter would normally reach the company by post – namely, two days after posting in the case of first class mail and after four days by second class mail.

The summons that is sent to the defendant tells him that he should file an admission of the claim or a defence (this means completing the printed form sent with the summons and sending it to the court) within 14 days from the date of service.

If the defendant does nothing, the plaintiff is entitled to seek judgment once the 14 days have expired. (Make a note of this date.) The plaintiff will not be told by the court that no defence has been filed, but if one is filed, a copy will be sent to him. This means that in the case of a default summons, the plaintiff merely has to add 14 days to the date of service inserted in the plaint note to know when he is able to seek judgment if no defence is filed.

seeking judgment in default

All that is needed is for the plaintiff to complete a 'request for entry of judgment' (form N.14). You can get a copy of the form from the court office (you can ask for it when you are getting the request form for a summons). Send it, together with the plaint note, to arrive at the court on or after the 14th day after the date given in the plaint note as the date of service of the summons. No fee is payable.

The court office will check whether a defence has been received.

If a defence is received by the court office after the 14 days but before your request for judgment is received, the court will accept it and the case will proceed as defended. In effect, while you cannot apply for judgment for 14 days, the defendant will be allowed to file a defence at any time until the court has acted on your application to enter judgment.

If no defence has been received, judgment will be entered in your favour – you will have won. The plaint note will be returned to you by the court with the date of judgment entered on it. You will then be entitled to enforce the judgment.

The court only notifies the defendant if payment is to be by instalments or by some future date. If the plaintiff wants judgment payable in full forthwith, it is up to him to notify the defendant and he can enforce straightaway.

Even in a case of judgment in default, the defendant may apply to have the decision set aside – and may succeed if he can show that he has a good defence to the claim.

judgments

There are two forms of judgment, usually called 'final' and 'interlocutory'. You can obtain final judgment where you are claiming a fixed amount – for example, £650 for repairs to your car. Where you are also claiming general damages – for example, for personal injuries – the amount will have to be assessed by the court. A 'request for interlocutory judgment for damages to be assessed' (form N.234) has to be completed. There will then need to be a hearing before a judge or registrar for him to decide the amount.

the defendant admits claim

The defendant may complete the form of 'admission, defence and counterclaim' sent to him with the summons to show that he admits the whole or part of the amount you claim. He may also make proposals about how and when the sum admitted will be paid. If he wishes to offer payment by a certain date or by weekly or monthly instalments, he must answer questions on the form as to his income and expenditure.

the amount admitted

You, the plaintiff, will be sent by the court a copy of the defendant's form of admission, together with another form (N.225) asking whether

(a) you accept the amount admitted and the proposal for payment, *or*
(b) you accept the amount admitted but not the proposal for payment, *or*
(c) you do not accept the part-amount admitted.

If the amount admitted is less than you claimed, you should weigh up the difference between your full claim and the amount admitted against the nuisance and cost to yourself in proceeding to a full hearing and the risk even then of not recovering the full amount claimed.

The second consideration is the method of payment. Again, you must weigh up the delay caused by payment by instalments against possible complications if you insist on getting payment in full without delay.

If you accept the amount admitted and also the method of payment, write to the court and say so (enclosing the plaint note) and judgment will be entered accordingly.

If you accept the amount admitted but not the method of payment, write to the court and say so and the court will fix a 'disposal' hearing.

If you do not accept the amount admitted, the case will proceed as a fully defended action, but you might be able to obtain a part judgment for the amount admitted.

part judgment

A part judgment is – as the name implies – a judgment for part only of the amount that is claimed, with the balance of the claim still to be decided.

For example, you claim payment for work done and say that, based on the number of hours worked, £400 is due. The defendant says that you gave a quotation for £250 for the work. You dispute this, saying either that no quotation was given or that you did extra work. There is a dispute about £150 which the court must resolve, but there is no dispute that you are owed £250. So, the registrar on a preliminary hearing might say "Part judgment for plaintiff for £250, the balance of the claim referred to arbitration."

The advantage of this is that you can take steps to enforce the part judgment without waiting for the decision as to the balance. Moreover, if the part judgment reduces the balance of the claim to below £500, it is likely that the registrar will allow arbitration, even though the automatic arbitration provisions do not strictly apply.

disposal hearing
If there is dispute only as to the method of payment, the court will fix a 'disposal' hearing. This is a short hearing (about 5 minutes or less) before a registrar at which he enters judgment for the amount admitted and decides how it is to be paid.

You, the plaintiff, are entitled to attend and would be wise to do so, so that you can question the defendant about his means and expenditure as stated on the form of admission. You may be able to show that he can afford more, and ask the registrar to make an order for higher instalments.

If the defendant does not turn up (as is often the case), you may be able to persuade the registrar to order payment immediately or within, say, 14 days. It is not always realistic, however, to try to extract the whole debt from the defendant in a lump sum: it may well be better to accept an offer of payment by instalments.

the defendant counterclaims

The form of 'admission, defence and counterclaim' can be used by the defendant to make a claim against the plaintiff, by writing in the amount he wants to claim and stating the reasons as if completing a particulars of claim.

If the defendant has filed a counterclaim, the registrar normally orders that the plaintiff files a defence to the counterclaim, setting out his grounds for disputing it. The registrar normally allows two to three weeks for this to be done.

The counterclaim will be heard in parallel with the plaintiff's claim. There is no court fee unless the amount counterclaimed is so much larger as to bring it into a higher court fee category.

defended action

On the form of 'admission, defence and counterclaim', the defendant who disputes the claim has to state his reasons and the amount he disputes.

the preliminary hearing

If the defendant files a defence – or the plaintiff does not accept a part admission – the court considers whether there is to be a preliminary hearing (also called a 'pre-trial review'). The practice of courts varies considerably: some automatically fix a preliminary hearing; in some, the papers are referred to a registrar who decides whether there should be a preliminary hearing or whether to refer the case directly to arbitration; or the registrar may give written directions instead, to ensure that the case is got ready for a hearing.

Where solicitors are involved or where the issues are relatively straightforward, there may not be a preliminary hearing.

The purpose of the preliminary hearing is to ensure that the issues in the case are clear, to record such agreement as there is between the parties in order to limit the issues that have to be decided at trial or arbitration, and to give such directions as are appropriate to ensure that the action is got ready for trial. Although the preliminary hearing may last only about 5 minutes, it is an important part of the proceedings.

When you are sent the defendant's completed form of defence, the court will also send you

* an appointment for a preliminary hearing, or
* a reference to arbitration – possibly with a date fixed, or
* written directions.

A preliminary hearing normally takes place in the registrar's chambers – his room – and the public are not admitted. Only the plaintiff and defendant and/or their representatives (if any) attend.

directions?

You should bring with you all documents relating to the case. Do not bring any witnesses with you – but you should have thought about whom you wish to call as witnesses, and whether expert evidence will be needed, so that you can tell the registrar.

You will need to assess whether your opponent has given you adequate particulars of the nature of his case and the facts (but not detailed evidence) on which he relies, and whether your opponent has documents in his possession that you need to see, so that both sides and the registrar know what still needs to be done.

further particulars

If the facts relied on are inadequately 'pleaded' – set out in the particulars of claim or defence – either party can write to the other asking him or her to supply further particulars (keep a copy of the letter).

If, for example, the plaintiff says simply that the defendant agreed to do something, the defendant may wish to know whether the plaintiff says that the agreement was oral or written: if oral, where, when and between whom the agreement was made; if written, he may want the document identified. This can be important: much time can be wasted if each party is thinking of a different agreement.

If an initial approach by letter for such particulars does not produce the required information, the court can be asked for an order that such particulars be provided within a fixed period. This can be done either at the preliminary hearing or by applying on form N.244 ('notice of application') obtainable from the court. A time for the hearing of the application before the registrar will be fixed. If the registrar considers that the particulars sought are necessary, he will order that the particulars are given in writing within so-many days (usually 14 or 21). The party ordered to give the particulars should send a copy to the other party and file one copy at the court office.

discovery of documents

It is a requirement that each party should disclose to the other at a relatively early stage in the proceedings the documents which are or have been in that party's possession which are in any sense relevant to the proceedings. This is known as 'discovery'. Exceptions to this rule are documents which are 'privileged': primarily, correspondence between a party and his or her solicitor, an expert's report prepared for the purpose of the proceedings, the advice or opinion of counsel.

If a document falls within a discoverable class, you have a duty to disclose it even if it is unhelpful to your case. The object of discovery is that each side should come to court with knowledge of the documents on which the other side intends to rely.

The county court rules envisage that each party should prepare the list of documents if asked for without any order from the court and that an order should be made only if a party fails to comply with a request for discovery. However, in practice, an order for discovery is given as a matter of course at the preliminary hearing if there is one. If not, and an order for discovery is required, an application can be made on the same form of notice as for further particulars (N.244).

The formal way of giving discovery is for each party to prepare a list of all such documents. There is a form for this, N.265, obtainable from county court offices. This divides relevant documents into

* documents now in the party's possession or control (he may not physically have them but is able to obtain possession of them)
* documents which are privileged
* documents which were in the party's possession or control but are no longer (for example, original letters sent to the other party).

The list should be prepared in triplicate, one copy being sent to the court, one to the other side and one kept for reference.

The other party is entitled to inspect and take copies of the documents, after fixing a convenient appointment to do so.

Discovery is not always necessary – at least, not in any formal sense. Many cases do not involve any significant number of documents and such that there are, are often common to both parties. In practice, in simple cases discovery consists of providing the other party with copies of relevant documents.

It is important that all relevant documents are disclosed well before the hearing. If at the hearing one party refers to a document that has not been disclosed, the other party may be able to have the case adjourned. He can ask for an order (even in an arbitration) that the party who referred to the document should pay the costs 'thrown away' – that is, the costs of his opponent attending court on that day and the immediate preparation for it.

expert evidence

The directions given at a preliminary hearing often call for expert evidence. If there is a dispute about the quality of building work, for example, evidence from a chartered surveyor or architect may be needed.

The general rule is that neither party can be called upon to disclose details of their witnesses – let alone the contents of their evidence – before the final hearing, but in the case of expert evidence, it is important that each side knows what the other side's experts have to say. This knowledge often leads to sensible settlements, at a considerable saving of time and money.

Where expert evidence is required, the court can order the disclosure of expert reports to the other side, within a fixed time. Send the report to your opponent and ask him to let you know if he is prepared to agree it. If he does so, the contents of the report are put before the judge as being agreed between the parties – even though there may be argument as to the effect or interpretation of what is said in the report.

If the expert's report is not agreed, the court will usually limit the number of expert witnesses that can be called to one or two, whose main evidence must be contained in the report that has been disclosed.

An attempt to call expert evidence at the hearing where a written report from that expert has not been disclosed in accordance with the registrar's directions, is likely to be refused by the judge or, alternatively, to lead to an adjournment with an order that the party calling the expert should pay the costs 'thrown away'.

directions for setting-down

The registrar at the preliminary hearing will try to assess when the case will be ready for trial and how long it will take. He will need to know that all the relevant documents are available, that they can be disclosed quickly, the number of witnesses to be called, that statements have been taken from witnesses, that experts – where required – have or can shortly prepare reports. In short, he will want to be satisfied that the case is nearly ready for hearing or can be made so quite quickly. If so, he directs that the court office fix a date for the hearing.

If this information is not available at this stage, the registrar will direct that when the information he requires is available, one or both parties should apply that a date for the hearing be fixed. He usually directs that the party who applies confirms that he or she is ready for hearing and gives an estimate of the length of time the hearing should take. Estimating the length of a hearing is notoriously difficult even for experienced lawyers. Probably the only thing that a layman can do is to indicate how many witnesses are to be called by each side, and leave the court to make an estimate of the length of the hearing.

judgment at preliminary hearing

It is possible for judgment to be given or the case to be dismissed at the preliminary hearing.

If the plaintiff but not the defendant appears at the preliminary hearing, the registrar may give judgment against the defendant, provided he is satisfied that there is no substance in what is said in the defendant's defence. He will also want some evidence from the plaintiff to show that the sum claimed is due.

Even if the defendant does attend, the plaintiff may be able to persuade the registrar that the defendant has not shown any genuine defence to the claim. This may be because the defence is not valid as a matter of law or because it is frivolous or prejudicial or an abuse of the process of the court. In these circumstances, however, it is more likely that an order will be made giving the defendant time to file a more adequate defence.

summary judgment

If the sum claimed exceeds £500, the plaintiff may seek 'summary judgment'. For this, a notice of application (N.244) must be completed asking for summary judgment. This, together with an affidavit in support, must be served on the defendant at least 7 days before the preliminary hearing or by a specified date. The affidavit can be on form N.285. It should set out relevant evidence, state that the contents of the particulars of claim are true, that the money claimed is still owing and also answer any points made in the defence, indicating why it is alleged that there is no defence to the claim. A solicitor's help in drafting the affidavit may be useful. The document has to be sworn before a solicitor or a court officer.

At the hearing of the application, the registrar will assess whether there is any issue that should come to trial. If he feels that there is no real defence in law or on the facts, he can give judgment for the plaintiff for all or part of the claim. If not, or if he gives judgment for part only, he will give directions for trial or arbitration.

judgment for the defendant

The defendant may be able to bring the action to an end either because the plaintiff does not turn up (in which case, unless some good reason has been given, the registrar may 'strike out' the plaintiff's claim) or because the particulars of claim disclose no reasonable grounds for the claim. For example, if a driver involved in a road accident sues not the other driver but his insurance company, the claim against the insurance company would be dismissed.

If the plaintiff's claim is struck out because the plaintiff did not attend rather than dismissed after a hearing between the parties, the plaintiff is entitled to apply to the court (on notice of application N.244) to restore the action. If a reasonable excuse for non-attendance is given, the plaintiff will probably succeed – but may have to pay costs 'thrown away'. Application should be made as quickly as possible once the plaintiff is aware of what has happened.

arbitration?

A claim for £500 or less routinely goes to arbitration, but if either party wants to have the action heard in open court, the preliminary hearing is the occasion to apply for this. Conversely, if the claim is for more than £500 and one party wants it to be heard by arbitration, then this is the time to ask for this to be agreed.

applying for further orders

Whether or not there has been a preliminary hearing, you can apply to the court for further orders. You might, for example, want to arrange for an expert to inspect work done at the other party's premises and have difficulty in arranging this with him. Or you might want the other party to produce original documents at the hearing, or, in a dispute over the merchantable quality of a car, for example, the defendant might want an order that the plaintiff make the car available for inspection.

It is sensible to write to your opponent asking him to agree to give you access. If he does not reply or will not agree, you apply for an order by completing the standard form of application (N.244) in triplicate. Send all three copies of the application to the court.

You can ask, for example, for "an order that the defendant allow the plaintiff's expert witness access to the defendant's premises in order to inspect the work done".

The court will fix a date for the application to be heard and return one or two of the copies to you. Technically, it is your responsibility to serve the notice of application on your respondent two clear working days before the hearing, but often the court does this. You must check to ensure that the court has done so. If not, you must serve the notice of application (by post) yourself.

At the hearing, the registrar either dismisses the application or makes the order that has been requested.

non-compliance

If your opponent fails to comply with a direction or order of the court, the most appropriate step is to complete a notice of application (N.244) asking the court for an order that unless the defendant complies within a fixed period, he be debarred from defending. Once a 'debarring order' is made, the plaintiff is entitled to apply for judgment in default of compliance – the same as if a defence had never been filed. If it is the plaintiff who has failed to comply, the registrar can be asked to order that the claim be struck out in default of compliance, and the action is then at an end.

Even if the defaulting party does not comply, the registrar may not make the order to debar or strike out if, for example, in the case of an application for discovery, it was clear that the other party had no documents of significance to disclose.

preparing for a hearing

The final preparations are similar whether
the hearing is to be in open court or by
arbitration.

The first step is to comply with the registrar's
directions and to provide any further particulars or
produce documents that have been ordered.

Then you need to consider your case again and
your opponent's defence. To know what facts you
have to prove in order to succeed in your case, you
may well need further information as to the law, from
a solicitor or citizens advice bureau or law centre.

The court will notify both the plaintiff and defendant of the date fixed
for the hearing. In general, if the date is not convenient for some good
reason, you should write in promptly, explain the problem and ask for
another date, telling the court of any date you cannot manage over the
month or so after the date originally fixed. The court office will alter the
original date if the other party agrees. If not, the matter will be referred
to the registrar.

alerting witnesses

Once the hearing date is finally fixed, both parties should tell their
witnesses, and make sure they can come to court on that day.

If a witness is reluctant, arrange for the court office to issue a witness
summons. Form N.286 – request for summons to witness – needs to be
completed and sent or taken to the court together with the fee (£8.50, or
£6 for a police officer) plus an amount for the witnesses' reasonable
travelling expenses from home or place of work to the court and back.
The witness summons can be served personally or be sent through the
post by the court at least 7 days before the hearing date.

You can ask anyone who has firsthand knowledge of any part of the
matter under dispute to be your witness. Go to see the person, find out
how much he or she knows, and make a note of the answers to your
questions or, preferably, get the person to make a written statement.

witness' statement

In most cases, a witness' statement is for your eyes only. The point of getting written statements is partly to have a record for your own information of what each witness can say and to check whether they do in fact corroborate your case. Make sure that the statement contains everything that the witness can tell you about the case and that it covers the points you wish to raise. It is easier to see possible weaknesses in the evidence if it is written down. You can then try to find ways of strengthening weak areas by asking the witness for more information or considering whether other witnesses are available.

Also, by asking the witness to give you a statement, you can help him remember what happened and get it clear in his mind. Neither you nor your witness will be able to refer to a statement when giving evidence except for any notes made contemporaneously with the incident to which you are referring or immediately afterwards.

If, for some reason, a witness will not be available to give evidence at an arbitration or hearing, you may persuade the registrar to take into account a written statement. It is therefore important that the statement gives the name and address of the witness, sets out his evidence in a sensible order (usually chronological) in as much detail as possible and is signed and dated by the witness. But a written statement carries far less weight than a witness in person.

expert witnesses

An expert witness is one who is not an eye witness but who gives evidence of expert opinion, based usually on an examination of the subject matter in dispute – whether that be the plaintiff's leg in the case of a road accident or the plaintiff's car where it is claimed that it was not of merchantable quality.

In a case of any substance where there are technical issues involved, the judge or registrar hearing the case – even if he does know something about the technical matters in issue – is not entitled to rely on his own knowledge but must make his decision on the basis of the evidence before him.

For instance, in a case involving a building dispute, what is wanted is the evidence of a surveyor or architect as to what is wrong with the work done, what is needed to put it right and the cost of so doing. In disputes over cars, a report from an AA or RAC engineer or other automobile engineer can be obtained. In disputes over domestic appliances, there may be a trade testing station which can give a report (a citizens advice bureau may have information about this).

A general rule about expert witnesses is that you should get them to inspect the subject matter of the dispute as early as possible. This has two advantages. First, they can give more contemporaneous evidence. A motor engineer's evidence as to the condition of a car is more valuable if he examined it within a few weeks of purchase than if he did not see it until a year later: questions would inevitably arise as to whether the car has deteriorated in the meanwhile and whether the alleged defects were present at the time of sale. Secondly, however strongly you feel about your case and the justice of your claim (or defence), the expert witness may not support you. You can at that stage get other expert advice but if your claim is technically a weak one, the sooner you are told the better – to discover at the last minute that your expert witness is not going to support your case may well lead to your having to discontinue the claim and pay your opponent's costs.

An expert's report is a privileged document if it has been brought into existence solely with regard to the matters that are in dispute in the action. (If a report is not favourable, you can withhold it, instruct another expert and use that expert's report if it is more favourable.) There is no general obligation to disclose any expert report you have commissioned, but you cannot produce expert evidence at the hearing if you have not previously disclosed that expert's written report. You must – if you wish to use an expert's report or call the expert as a witness – disclose the report to the other side. Your opponent may find out that you have had the subject matter of the dispute inspected by more than one expert, and he is entitled to cross-examine you at the hearing on why you obtained two reports of which only one has been produced – and this can be very damaging for you. Or he can issue a witness summons (subpoena) to the first expert, who must then give evidence as to what he saw on his inspections and his views of the matter in issue, even though his actual report remains a privileged document.

Expert evidence can be expensive. The cost of an expert's report must be borne by the person obtaining it. To avoid the full effect of this, it may be worth asking your opponent if he will agree jointly to appoint an expert. This does not prevent either of you from later calling further evidence to challenge the evidence of the jointly instructed expert, but it saves costs initially.

If your opponent disagrees with the report, you should warn the expert that he should be ready to attend court and give evidence in due course.

documents

Each side should have prepared a list of documents and sent this to the other. You should arrange to inspect any documents that are not already known to you and obtain copies of any that have any significance. (You must pay the copying charges incurred by your opponent in supplying you with the copies.) In most cases, it is best to prepare a bundle of all the documents which the two sides agree as relevant to the issue and accept as valid.

Four identical page-numbered bundles of legible photocopies are needed – for the judge or registrar, the witness and each side. The originals should be available for production because, generally, documents which are copies are not acceptable in evidence in open court. If both parties agree a copy document to go in the bundle of documents, there is no problem. If, for any reason, it is not agreed, and the original document is in your opponent's possession, you should serve a 'notice to produce' the original of the document (form N.284). If your opponent does not produce the original, you are then entitled to produce a copy of the document. Have four copies of the copy ready for use in court as well as the 'original' copy.

If the original document is not agreed and is not in your opponent's possession, the only course is to issue a witness summons to the person who has the document, to attend court and bring the document with him.

If there are any documents whose validity is disputed, these should not be included in the bundle. The person who wants to produce any disputed documents should serve on the other party a 'notice to admit' (form N.283). The effect of this is that that party is called upon to admit the validity of the document within 7 days. If he does not do so, he will have to pay the costs of your producing evidence to validate the document – whether or not you win the case.

Your opponent may not specifically have admitted in the pleadings a fact which is essential to your case even though it may not be in dispute. For example, the terms of an agreement might be pleaded in the particulars of claim and yet the defendant has neither disputed nor admitted such terms. To prove them satisfactorily might involve calling additional witnesses who might not otherwise be necessary. The expense of so doing can be avoided by serving a 'notice to admit facts' (form N.281) which operates in much the same way as a notice to admit documents. If the other party does not admit the facts as set out in the notice within 7 days, you will be entitled to the costs of successfully proving the facts, whether or not you succeed in the claim.

example

Alan Jones bought a secondhand Metro from Bob White. The car broke down and needed extensive repairs within a week. Alan wants to sue Bob for the cost of the breakdown repairs, the cost of putting the car into good condition or the difference in value of the car, incidental expenses and damages for loss of use of the car.

Bob had advertised the car as "immaculate" and, when Alan inspected the car, Bob also stated that the engine was in excellent condition and that the car had done only 9,000 miles. If Alan had said "I offer you £1,400 for the car on the basis that the engine is in good condition and that the car has done only 9,000 miles" and Bob had accepted this, these statements would have been part of the contract and Alan could sue for breach of contract.

Unless any of these statements had been specifically included in Alan's offer to buy the car, Alan would have to rely on the law as to misrepresentation. Assuming that there is no question of fraud on Bob's part, Alan will have to claim that a false representation was made, on which he relied, which caused him the amount of loss he is claiming.

Bob can defend by disputing any of these points: for example, that the description "immaculate" was a mere advertising puff and was not intended as a representation and that Alan had not seemed to think that it was. Perhaps he might also allege that Alan had brought with him a mechanic who carried out an inspection (so that Alan had therefore not relied on the representation). Or Bob can prove that he believed the representation to be true and that he had reasonable grounds for so believing.

Alan has to prove
- that each of the statements was made
- that they were representations
- that he relied on them
- that they were false to a material degree

and also

- that he has suffered loss as a result, and how much.

Alan's proof
To prove the making of the statements, Alan will need a copy of the advertisement.

He can give his own evidence about the oral statements but should call anyone else who was present when the conversation took place who can remember clearly what was said and is prepared to make a statement.

Evidence by a witness may help to establish that the statements were made by Bob in such a way that they were intended to induce Alan to make the contract. For example, a witness to Bob's statement that the car had done only 9,000 miles and his claim that the engine was in excellent condition might say:

> "Jim Cole of 9 Beech Avenue, Anytown, states:
> I am a friend of Alan Jones.
> At his request, I went with him to Bob White's house at 42 Cedar Drive, Anytown in the afternoon of 15th March 1985.
> Alan and I inspected the car. It seemed in good condition. Alan asked Bob about the condition of the engine. We were all sitting in the car at the time, Alan and Bob in front, I was sitting in the back. Bob said that the engine was in excellent condition. Alan also looked at the mileage recorder and asked whether the mileage shown was correct. Bob said "yes". I did not see what the mileage reading was then.
> After this conversation, Alan offered £1,400 for the car. Bob would not accept – he said that the car had done only 9,000 miles and that the engine and bodywork were in excellent condition. Eventually Alan offered £100 more and Bob accepted it.
> About a week later, I went out for a drive with Alan in the car. We had gone only about 15 miles when the oil pressure light came on, there was a smell of overheating and, before Alan could get the car to the roadside, it stopped. We pushed it to the side of the road and Alan phoned a breakdown service. While he was doing so, I made a note of the mileage reading. This was exactly 9,100. Then the breakdown truck came and the car was towed to a garage."
> Signed: JIM COLE date: 6 April 1985.

Alan himself will need to prove that he relied on the representations. His own statement that he did so will be sufficient unless Bob can show that this is not correct. For example, if Alan – before buying the car – got an AA or RAC engineer's report, the court would be unlikely to accept that Alan had relied in any effective way on Bob's representations as to the condition of the car.

Alan will then need to show that the representations were false. He can do this in part by factual evidence – that the car broke down after only 50 miles driving. For a car over 3 years old, a MoT certificate would show the car's recorded mileage.

Alan will almost certainly also need to obtain a report from a motor engineer as to the condition of the engine and the likely mileage that it has done. The engineer should state what work needs to be done to put the engine into reasonable condition and, if possible, give information as to the likely cost of labour and parts. He will also need to give evidence as to the value of the car at its likely actual mileage compared with the 9,000 miles that it was represented to have done.

Alan should then send to Bob a list of documents (or copies of documents), such as

(a) the advertisement
(b) bill of sale or receipt for the car
(c) bills for any work done to the engine
(d) any documents establishing the mileage that the car has done
(e) any documents handed over to him by Bob when he bought the car
(f) correspondence between Alan and Bob
(g) estimates for further repairs.

The motor engineer's expert report is not in the list of documents to be disclosed but Alan sends a copy of it to Bob and asks whether he agrees the contents of the report.

If Bob disputes the report, he can say that he wishes the engineer to attend the hearing as an expert witness. Bob should also be asked whether he agrees that the cost of repairs is reasonable; if not, a witness may have to be called to give evidence about that.

Bob may ask Alan to give further and better particulars of his claim: for example, full details of each representation that was given; when made; whether written or oral; if written, identifying the document; if oral, stating when and where said, by whom and to whom. Alan should respond to this request as accurately as possible.

When all this is done, if a date for the arbitration has not already been fixed, Alan should write to the court and ask for a date to be fixed. He should tell the court how many witnesses he is going to call (this helps the court office to estimate the length of the hearing).

arbitration hearing

An arbitration hearing is generally held in the registrar's chambers – this is usually a largish room with the registrar's desk at one end and at right angles to this, a table with chairs on both sides. The plaintiff and his witnesses sit on one side, the defendant and his witnesses on the other. In some courts, the hearing may be held in the court room, but an arbitration hearing is normally not open to the public. Either party can be represented by a solicitor or, at the discretion of the registrar, any other adviser.

Make sure you bring with you all the documents and papers relevant to your case, in accessible order.

The procedure in arbitration varies not only from court to court but also between different cases. The registrar takes charge of the proceedings. He has to conduct them in such a way as to enable him to discover the facts of the specific case and to make a decision.

The registrar may start by explaining briefly the procedure he is going to adopt. He will then ask the plaintiff to explain his or her case, and will probably ask questions until he is clear in his mind about the plaintiff's case.

The registrar will then probably ask the defendant if he or she wishes to ask questions of the plaintiff. If, instead of questions, the defendant simply makes comments on the plaintiff's evidence, the registrar may be able to convert such comments into questions, or he may get the defendant to state his or her case and will then question the defendant in the same way as he questioned the plaintiff. Arising out of this, he may ask the plaintiff more questions.

witnesses

If there are witnesses, the registrar generally questions them himself. Make it clear to the registrar once you have given evidence yourself that you have witnesses to call and ask when he would like them to give evidence. He may hear their evidence before the defendant, or may prefer to hear the defendant's case before hearing witnesses from either side.

Generally witnesses come in with the parties, but there are courts where it is the practice to keep them out (sometimes for reasons of space). Some registrars prefer witnesses in particular cases, such as road accidents or cases where a lot turns on the credibility of witnesses to remain outside so that they do not hear what the parties say. This is the rule in criminal courts, but not in civil courts.

registrar's decision
When the registrar feels that he has got all the facts clear, he will probably ask the defendant first, then the plaintiff, whether they wish to say any more. After that, he gives his judgment (technically this is an award, which is entered at the court as a judgment).

The registrar usually gives this in some detail, with his reasons for coming to the decision, and does not simply say "judgment for the plaintiff for £400". What he orders may be less than the amount claimed if he thinks the amount was unreasonable or that the plaintiff was partly to blame. Both plaintiff and defendant get a copy of the order. It is important to retain this.

claiming expenses

The successful party is entitled to claim his expenses in attending court for the arbitration, but not the cost of attending the preliminary hearing nor of any other journeys to the court. He can also claim the expenses of his witnesses in attending court to give evidence, and the court fee (if he is the plaintiff), and any other out-of-pocket expenses in preparing the case, such as photocopying, fares and telephone calls needed to get together evidence, and experts' fees.

He should ask for an order for expenses to be paid by the loser when the registrar has given judgment and should, where possible, produce written evidence of his lost wages (net of tax and of national insurance contributions) and of his travelling expenses. It is up to the registrar how much of the winner's claim for expenses the loser should be ordered to pay.

If the arbitration is for more than £500, the successful party can seek – and will usually obtain – an order for his legal costs, as well as his expenses, to be paid by his opponent. For a litigant in person, this means that he can claim for his time spent in preparing his case and in attending court (including the preliminary hearing). He is entitled to claim the actual loss that he has suffered or, if he cannot show a specific financial loss, he can charge £6 per hour but is not entitled to recover more than two-thirds of what a solicitor would be allowed.

paying up

Do not throw away or lose any of the documents relating to the case (for example, the plaint note, the certificate of judgment) because you may need to produce them or to refer to them if you have to go back to the court for an order to enforce payment.

The unsuccessful party may wish to apply to the registrar for an order to pay the judgment by instalments instead of in a lump sum. He should do this as soon as the question of costs and expenses is sorted out at the end of the arbitration. It is important to bring along evidence of earnings (such as recent pay slips) and outgoings – rent book, mortgage statements, rates demands, HP repayment books and so on. The registrar can then assess a realistic amount for weekly or monthly payments.

If payment is not by instalments, the full amount must be paid forthwith' or in a number of days' time (perhaps fourteen).

hearing in open court

There is no essential difference between preparing a case for a hearing in open court or for an arbitration hearing. But hearings in open court are subject to normal rules of procedure and evidence; more care is therefore needed to make sure that everything is in order. If it is found at the hearing that further evidence is required, or that documents are not available or cannot properly be proved, an adjournment is unlikely to be granted or, if granted, there is a strong chance that you will be ordered to pay your opponent's costs 'thrown away' – that is, his additional costs in having to come on that day without getting the case resolved. Since it is likely that your opponent will have legal representation, these costs may be quite high.

It may be wise to get at least some legal advice before the hearing. For this, prepare a full, but reasonably succinct, account of your case and take all relevant documents with you, including pleadings, orders and any other court documents, so that you do not find yourself having to pay for time wasted while the solicitor tries to get the case clear before being able to advise you.

In open court, witnesses will not be allowed to read their evidence from a note (or 'proof of evidence') except expert witnesses. Nonetheless, it is helpful to prepare for yourself a summary of the evidence that you and each witness can give. To prepare the evidence for your side, write out your own statement and also speak to and obtain statements from anyone whom you may wish to call as a witness. This enables you to check that the evidence does cover all the points that you need to prove and also has the advantage of helping your witnesses to recall what happened and get their evidence clearly in their minds in a logical order. Such statements should be among the papers you take with you if you seek legal advice.

payment into court

It is not uncommon for the defendant, during the preparation of the case for hearing, to pay into court part of the sum claimed in settlement and to give notice of this to the plaintiff. (The judge is never told about a payment into court prior to giving judgment.)

The plaintiff has 14 days from the date of notice of payment-in to accept the payment in settlement of the action. If he does accept (perhaps after further negotiation with the defendant), he has to notify the court. This ends the case.

If he does not accept and the judge eventually gives judgment to the plaintiff for a sum equal to or less than the amount paid into court, the defendant is entitled to be paid his costs from the date of payment-in onwards and the plaintiff entitled to his costs only up to that date.

Costs after the payment-in would include the costs of the hearing itself, so a plaintiff can be at risk for hefty costs if he does not accept the payment-in.

example
The plaintiff claims £1,000 for the cost of remedying unsatisfactory building work. The defendant pays in £500 at the time he files his defence. The plaintiff does not accept – running the risk of having to pay all the costs of the defendant in instructing expert witnesses, arranging for them to inspect the work, instructing counsel, preparing the case for hearing and attending court for a day or more. The costs of this could be £1,500 or more.

The judge in the end decides that the defendant's workmanship entailed remedial work of no more than £450. The plaintiff receives £450 plus his costs to the date of payment-in (a relatively small sum), but has to pay the defendant's costs of £1,500+.

It is therefore important to consider very seriously any payment-in, in the light of possible costs; it is probably wise to seek legal advice.

final preparations

Before going to court, you should read again your own pleadings and those of your opponent. If you are a plaintiff, make a note of the various points that you have to prove to succeed in your case and of the witnesses or documents covering each point. If you are the defendant, you will need to see what documents or witnesses will help you in defeating the plaintiff's evidence on the points he has to prove.

See what your opponent's case is from the pleadings and try to work out what he will say in evidence. You can then prepare the bones of cross-examination, the flesh coming when you are actually in court. Try to anticipate all possible angles of the case, even if they are unlikely, and prepare for them. The one aspect you do not prepare for is likely to be the one you will be asked about.

Evidence which does not relate to relevant points, at least in part, is just wasted time and effort. Although you will not directly suffer by calling irrelevant evidence, it will not impress the judge and may waste time and incur costs. A judge will, in particular, have little sympathy with attempts to bring in extraneous matters just to score off your opponent.

procedure in open court

In most cases, the procedure will take the following course.

The clerk of the court calls out the name of the case – "Smith v Brown" – and hands the court file to the judge or registrar who is hearing the case.

The plaintiff then gets up, and when he has the judge's or registrar's attention, he should say words to the following effect: "I am the plaintiff in this case, my name is Walter Smith. I am conducting my own case. The defendant is also conducting his own case" (or "is represented by Mr Wolfe").

Before the hearing, find out the name of the opposing solicitor, if you do not already know it, and the opposing barrister, if there is one. You address the judge as 'your honour' and the registrar as 'sir' (or 'madam'). The cause list outside the court will tell you whether your case is being heard by a judge or registrar.

The plaintiff then 'opens' the case with a brief summary of the facts (as set out in the particulars of claim) underlying the case and of the evidence he will call. The purpose of this is to enable the judge to understand, before he hears evidence, what the case is all about.

example

In Alan and Bob's case, Alan as the plaintiff might say:

> "On the 15th of March 1985, I saw an advertisement in the Anytown Mercury of a secondhand Metro car for sale. It was described as being in immaculate condition. I arranged to inspect the car with my friend Jim Cole. I asked the defendant who was

selling the car what condition the engine was in. He said it was in very good condition. I then asked him what mileage the car had done. He pointed to the mileometer and said it had done 9,000 miles. In fact, the reading showed 9,051. Relying on those statements by the defendant, I decided to buy the car and paid the defendant £1,500. I took the car away the following day. After I had had it only a few days and had driven the car about 50 miles, the engine oil warning light suddenly came on and before I could stop the car, the engine seized up. The car was inspected by an engineer who said that the engine had severe oil leaks and that it had certainly done many more miles than 9,000 – at least twice as much. The cost of repairing the engine amounted to £450. I shall produce expert evidence to show that the value of a car with approximately 20,000 miles is £150 less than a car having done only 9,000 miles. While the car was off the road and being repaired, I hired another car in order to get to work. This cost £120. I therefore claim £720 together with interest from the date on which the car was repaired."

The plaintiff should then go through the defendant's defence indicating what points are agreed and what are disputed.

If there is an agreed bundle of documents, this should then be handed to the judge. It may be helpful to go through the bundle and point out to the judge the more significant documents – but keep it brief. Have your own copy bundle of documents ready for immediate reference.

Both when making your opening statement and in giving your evidence, try to speak slowly and distinctly. If the judge is recording your remarks or evidence in his notebook, watch his pen and wait until he has caught up with you before proceeding. If you are giving evidence and are being asked questions by your opponent's counsel or solicitor, try to remember to turn to the judge to give your replies, as it is important that he hears what you say. Court acoustics are often far from perfect.

plaintiff's evidence

The evidence is then called in the following sequence.

• The plaintiff himself gives evidence in the witness box, after taking the oath or affirming.
• He calls other witnesses, in the order in which they became involved in the events in dispute. (This often means that the expert witness comes last.) Witnesses have to take the oath or affirm.

- Each witness gives evidence 'in chief' and is then cross-examined by the opposing party or that party's representative.
- After cross-examination, the party calling the witness has the right to re-examine to deal with any points that arose in cross-examination.

If the other party is not legally represented or if the judge feels that the evidence is confusing, the judge himself may intervene at any time to ask questions.

cross-examination

Cross-examination is difficult. It is an art that cannot really be taught but only acquired by experience.

Your aim will be to discredit the other side's story or argument. You should therefore try to prepare your cross-examination in advance, at least in note form. To do that, you have to work out what the case against you involves (from the pleadings or evidence that you have seen), decide how that will be presented and then decide how best to attack it, or at least to raise doubts as to whether your opponent's version is true.

Do not regard cross-examination as a chance to score points off your opponent: you may find that your opponent scores more points than you do.

Although not a rule of evidence, you should always be courteous and keep your temper. You may think that the witness is lying through his back teeth, but loss of temper or rudeness on your part is not likely to show this up.

A golden rule in cross-examination is: do not ask a question unless you have reason to think that the answer, if truthful, is going to help your case.

It is important to put to the opposing party the essential facts of your case so that he has the opportunity of admitting or denying them. For example, Alan should ask Bob "Did you not say that the car had done only 9,000 miles?" . . . "Did you not say that the engine was in very good condition?", etc.

Do not, however, ask too much. Decide on what points you need your opponent to answer and, when each point has been covered, leave it at that. Once all the points have been covered, sit down. When you have made your point, there is no advantage in going further because you may well ask one question too many to which the witness gives the wrong answer ('wrong' from your point of view, that is) destroying all your good work to date. An example of this is an apocryphal episode in a trial that took place some years ago. The case involved a road accident and the key witness for one side was a man who had seen the crash and had given an estimate of the speed at which one of the cars was travelling. Counsel for the defence established in cross-examination that the witness did not hold a driving licence, had never driven a car himself and indeed had no experience in judging the speed of cars. Counsel should have left it there but, no doubt flushed with success, went on to ask what the witness did for a living. It then came out that the witness was a train driver and as such was well used to judging the relative speeds of moving vehicles. The defendant lost. Bear that in mind when you are tempted to build on your victory. Once you have got what you want, then go on to the next point.

giving evidence
To a great extent, success usually depends on how well one's story can be put, and got across to the judge. A fair amount of latitude is given to the litigant in person, but you should make sure that your case proceeds in order, and that documents are readily available when required in court.

When the plaintiff in person gives evidence, he will have to do this without any notes, unless he can satisfy the judge that the notes were made contemporaneously, or nearly so, with the matters on which he is giving evidence. It is therefore important that, without learning his evidence parrot-fashion, the plaintiff should have clearly in his mind the sequence of the evidence that he has to give and the vital points that he must prove.

The plaintiff is then cross-examined by the other side.

When you are being cross-examined, do not get flustered, do not try to be clever and do not 'fence' with the questioner. Just answer the questions as briefly as possible, but make sure that you include everything in your answer that you feel is relevant. If you are interrupted, then insist on your right to reply in full to the question and, if necessary, ask the judge for permission to carry on. If you start arguing with your opponent or try to knock down his questions, you run the risk of being torn to shreds by any competent advocate who is likely to be a lawyer with far more experience than you at this sort of thing – and you also risk alienating the judge.

After cross-examination, there is no one to re-examine the plaintiff in person but he can give further evidence himself on any matter about which he has been asked in cross-examination. This does not mean just repeating what was said in his evidence 'in chief' but adding to it to deal with the points raised by his opponent.

The plaintiff's other witnesses are called in turn, take the oath or affirm, and the plaintiff questions them, using the statements he has previously taken from them. In questioning his own witnesses, the plaintiff must take care not to 'lead' them by suggesting the answer that he is hoping to get.

The defendant cross-examines the plaintiff's witnesses in turn, asking questions designed to weaken the plaintiff's case. The plaintiff can re-examine his witnesses on any points raised in cross-examination. Once a witness has left the box after re-examination, that is it: he or she cannot be recalled without special permission from the judge.

When the plaintiff has finished calling his evidence, he should say to the judge "That concludes my evidence, your honour."

Throughout the hearing, take notes of the evidence that has been given. It is difficult or impossible to do this while you are actually giving evidence or examining witnesses yourself and you must not take a tape recorder into court. So, if possible, ask a friend to come with you and to take the notes. The purpose of the notes is to have a record of what has been said so that if there is a dispute or an appeal later, the correct version can be established.

At any stage, if you are unsure as to what happens next or how you should proceed, ask the judge for guidance. He will not expect you to be an experienced advocate and should not mind giving you some assistance. Do not be afraid to ask.

the defendant's evidence

The defendant then gives evidence, pointing out the relevant facts. He then calls his various witnesses in turn.

The plaintiff has the right to cross-examine the other side's witnesses after they have given evidence; the defendant can then re-examine the witnesses. When he has finished calling his evidence, the defendant should say so.

final address

Once all the evidence has been given, each side has the chance to close his case by addressing the court. The closing speech should be kept brief and should deal with the law and the relevant parts of the evidence. Do not just rehash your case: that will not endear you to the judge. But you can mention particular items of evidence, particularly matters conceded by your opponent under cross-examination, which tend to support your case.

The judge has to decide, on the balance of probabilities, whether the plaintiff's account of what happened is more likely to be correct than the defendant's. You should draw to the judge's attention points that you think will show him that your own account is more probable than your opponent's. If, in the judge's view, both parties' cases are equal, the judge must dismiss the plaintiff's claim.

the judgment

The judge will then give his judgment. He may retire for a few minutes but in most cases makes his decision straightaway, giving the reasons why he has come to it. Take a note of what is said by the judge – preferably in full if you or a friend can manage shorthand. The point of taking a record is the possibility of an appeal.

The plaintiff and defendant will receive from the court a copy of the court order which incorporates the judge's decision.

If you are an unsuccessful defendant, now is the time to ask for an instalment order, so that you pay in set weekly or monthly amounts. Be ready to make a sensible offer – however aggrieved you feel at losing your case – and be prepared to provide documents showing your income and expenditure and to give oral evidence if the judge requires.

If the judge has given judgment in your favour, you should straightaway ask for costs so that these can be ordered at the same time. At the end of the trial, you may want to die of exhaustion, sit down or faint – but do not do any of these things until you have asked for costs.

costs

The term 'costs' when awarded, covers both repayment of money spent in bringing the case (such as court fees, payments to expert witnesses), and solicitors' charges for work done and counsel's fees.

At the end of an action in open court, the successful party is entitled to ask the court to order the other party to pay his costs. If the successful party asks, the judge can assess the amount of costs there and then. If not, the judge will order that the costs are 'taxed'. 'Taxing' by the court means that the bill has to be drawn up in a special way and the items are examined in detail to decide whether the charges made were fair and reasonable. The payer will have to pay the fee for taxation (5p for every £1 of the bill as taxed).

If you lost and an order for taxed costs is made against you, you are entitled to see a detailed bill showing the work that has been done by the other party's solicitor. This should show the charges for various steps in the proceedings, in accordance with scales laid down by the rules of court, including specific charges for various attendances at court and for the general preparation of the case. These charges are based on an hourly charge for the time spent, together with a figure for 'uplift' which is supposed to represent the solicitor's profit and also some compensation for the time which is spent on the case but has not been fully recorded by the solicitor.

The prepared bill is lodged with the court where the action was heard. The court will send a copy of the bill to the party who will have to pay, telling him that he is entitled to be present when the bill is taxed by the court's registrar, provided that he gives notice to the court within 14 days by letter, that he wants to do this.

If no such notice is given, the registrar provisionally taxes the bill – that is, makes sure that the amounts claimed are in accordance with the appropriate costs rules. If the solicitor lodging the bill accepts the registrar's provisional taxation, an order for payment of the amount as taxed is issued; this can be enforced as any other money judgment of the court.

If either the party who will have to pay asks to be heard on the taxation, or the solicitor objects to the provisional taxation, an appointment is fixed when the registrar hears what each side wants to say about the amount claimed and makes a decision about each item in dispute. After that, the order for costs is issued by the court.

the £500 threshold

Only in very exceptional circumstances will an unsuccessful party in arbitration proceedings where the amount claimed is less than £500 have to pay his opponent's legal costs. Costs can be awarded only where there has been unreasonable conduct on the part of the opposite party in relation to the proceedings. Generally, this means that the party ordered to pay the costs has caused the other party extra expenses by failing to produce documents or expert reports when ordered, or by failing to attend court for a hearing or by causing an unnecessary adjournment because of not having the evidence available which he should have had there.

Where the amount claimed is in excess of £500 (whether or not the eventual decision is for less than £500), the usual rules as to costs apply and the successful party is entitled to ask for his costs.

Where a case for over £500 is heard in open court, the winner will be allowed to ask for his costs even if the judgment is for less than £500. If, however, the judgment is for less than £500 and the judge thinks that there never was any real possibility of recovering more than £500 although the claim was for more, he might consider that the claim for over £500 was a sham designed simply to enable the case to be heard in open court so that the successful party could claim costs. For that reason, he may refuse to make an order for costs.

There is no right to costs: they normally 'follow the event' (loser pays) but the courts have a discretion – and use it.

the costs you can claim

A litigant in person is in general allowed £6 per hour for time reasonably spent in attending court and preparing his case. If you can show that you had actual financial loss in excess of £6 per hour in preparing your case, you can claim this, subject to a limit of two-thirds of what a solicitor could charge.

If the judge awards you costs, you can ask for him to assess them there and then or you can ask for them to be 'taxed' by the registrar of the court at a later hearing in chambers. For taxation, you will have to prepare a formal statement showing how your costs are calculated.

assessment of costs

If your costs are being assessed by the judge, you should tell him any out-of-pocket expenses you have had. Have ready an itemised list of your expenditure including court fees, fees for witness summonses, copying charges for documents, witnesses' expenses such as their loss of earnings in attending court, expert witnesses' fees, also essential travelling expenses. (From the moment your case starts and is given a number by the court, keep every bus ticket, note every stamp, phone call, photocopy etc.) Put all the items you think relevant on to the list – the judge will either allow or disallow.

The maximum that the judge can assess is based on the scale used for solicitors' costs, as follows:

claim (defendant) *or gain (plaintiff)**	*maximum assessed costs*
up to £500	£58
£500 to £3,000	£218
£3000+	£264

*Costs in the county court for the successful defendant are awarded according to what was claimed against him; for the successful plaintiff, according to what he actually gains.

Assessment by judge or registrar is inevitably at a far lower figure than taxation. You may find that the cost of your expert witness alone swallows up all the assessed costs allowed and therefore it may be in your interest to have the bill 'taxed', even though this means extra work.

enforcement of judgments

Obtaining a judgment in your favour may be easy enough in many cases, but this may be less than half the battle: obtaining the money may be much more difficult. The court will not do anything about it unless you take enforcement proceedings.

Where a claim turns out to have been against an individual who just does not have the money to meet the judgment or is adept at making use of all the court processes to avoid payment, you are going to have a difficult task to obtain payment in full.

You should try to discover whether the defendant is worth powder and shot before you spend time and money on seeking to enforce judgment. If a search of the register of attachment of earnings orders, at the county court for the area in which the debtor resides, shows a number of existing debts being enforced against the debtor, you may decide it is not worth your while to proceed.

A free booklet, *Enforcing money judgments in the county court*, available from county courts, explains the procedure for obtaining payment without employing a solicitor.

There are several methods of enforcement available which can be used once the time for payment has passed. Where the full amount of the judgment debt is payable by a certain date, you will have to wait for that date to pass before you can issue any form of enforcement of the judgment. If payment is by instalments, you cannot issue enforcement proceedings unless at least one payment is overdue.

But it is unwise to be optimistic about the outcome of trying to enforce payment.

warrant of execution

The most common method of enforcement is the warrant of execution. (A similar method is available in the High Court where it is called a writ of fieri facias – 'fi. fa.' for short. Where a county court judgment is for over £2,000, it is possible to transfer it to the High Court for enforcement by issue of a writ of fi. fa.)

A warrant of execution is an order for the court bailiff to seize sufficient of the person's goods as will, on sale by auction, discharge the debt shown on the warrant.

You have the choice of issuing a warrant for any instalment overdue (if £50 or more), or for the whole of the judgment debt, or for any amount in excess of £50.

If the whole debt is due in one payment, you can issue a warrant of execution for less than the full amount, as long as it is for at least £50. It can be effective to issue the warrant for less than the full amount because – faced with a warrant for a reasonably small amount – the debtor may pay up rather than have his possessions removed and sold. The very fact that you have taken steps to issue a warrant may indicate that you mean business and may encourage the debtor to keep up payments.

issuing the warrant

For a warrant of execution to be issued, you have to complete a request form (N.323) and send it or take it to the county court where you obtained judgment. Together with it, take the plaint note and the fee of 15p for every £1 for which the warrant is issued – minimum fee £5, maximum £30. The court office then issues the warrant.

If you have special information as to the defendant's goods – for example, where he garages his car away from his house – tell the court in writing when applying for the warrant to be issued.

enforcing the warrant

If the defendant lives within the area of the county court where you applied, the court's own bailiffs will act on the warrant. Otherwise, the warrant will be sent to the county court for the area within which the defendant lives (or carries on business) to be enforced by that court's bailiffs.

How long it will take the bailiff to deal with the warrant varies from court to court and depends on the number of warrants outstanding in that court at any particular time – delays of several weeks are common. If the bailiff is not able to deal with the warrant within one month, he should notify you of what has happened: the bailiff may have been unable to enter – he has no power to force entry into a private dwellinghouse (no such restriction for business premises). If the bailiff has been unable to enter, he will continue to make (up to, say, six) attempts to enter before finally giving up hope – and then so should you.

County court bailiffs are always overworked and any creditor is well advised to check regularly on a warrant's progress by telephoning early in the morning when bailiffs call to collect their day's work.

The bailiff may report that there are insufficient goods of the debtor's to cover the cost of removal and sale. Or he may say that goods have been seized with a view to sale – and you can hope to get some money in due course.

Unless there are assets of real value at the defendant's house, removal and sale of his possessions may not benefit you greatly. The cost of removing the goods and the commission payable to the auctioneer on the sale have to be deducted from the sale proceeds. You will get what is left and must set against that the fee you have paid for the issue of the warrant. Indeed, if there is a shortfall, you will have to pay the court the balance of the expenses.

It may be worth having a word with the bailiff first to discover what sort of goods are available for sale. He may well be able to give you some idea of what they would reach if sold by auction, and an estimate of the costs of removal and commission to be paid to the auctioneer.

suspended warrant
The defendant may respond to the issue of a warrant by making an application for the warrant to be suspended, promising to make weekly or monthly payments of an agreed figure. He will have to fill in a form giving brief details of his income and expenditure. The court will send you a copy so that you can make up your mind as to the reasonableness or otherwise of the offer that the defendant has made. Even an offer that appears ludicrous, entailing payments over a number of years before the debt is paid, should be given serious consideration. (While payment over a long period may seem unacceptable, the alternatives may not necessarily be any better.)

Weekly or monthly payments under a suspended warrant leave the warrant in being, ready to be enforced if the defendant fails to keep up payments. At the very least, there is a reasonable chance of some payments being made and the possibility of enforcing the warrant by sale if payments are not kept up.

If you are in doubt as to the accuracy of the information given by the defendant in making his application to pay by instalments, you should attend court when the defendant's application is heard and question him about his means. Write to the defendant in advance and ask him to produce to the court documentary evidence of his income (perhaps his last three payslips) and of his expenditure and commitments (rent book, HP repayment book, gas and electricity bills, court orders).

At the hearing, you can put any arguments you have about the method or amount of payments to the registrar. The one argument that is likely to fall on deaf ears is that it will take too many years for the debt to be paid off.

Debtors can frustrate enforcement by making repeated applications for suspension or setting aside. The registrar can be asked by the enforcer to order that the defendant's application to suspend be dismissed, and that no further similar applications should be allowed. Ask the registrar specifically to direct that the warrant shall proceed.

attachment of earnings order

Another fairly common method of enforcement is the issue of an application for an attachment of earnings order. This is an application to have a weekly or monthly sum directly deducted from the defendant's wages by his employer and paid to the court, which in turn pays it over to you.

The chief disadvantage is that such an order cannot be made in a case where the defendant is self-employed or out of work. Another disadvantage is that, by its very nature, the order entails payments over a period of time.

An application for an attachment of earnings order is made in the same way as an application for a warrant of execution: the debt must be due and payable under a judgment order, a request (in this case form N.337) has to be completed and sent to the court with the plaint note and fee – 10p per £ of the debt: minimum fee £5, maximum fee £30.

The court to apply to is the one for the area in which the defendant lives. If this is not the court where you obtained your judgment, you must first write to that court asking for the action to be transferred to the court for the area where the debtor lives, and the application, plaint note and fee are then sent to that court.

The form of request asks you to supply the name and address of the defendant's employers, if known to you. If you can supply this information, it will speed up the making of an order.

There will be a hearing and a notice of the application is sent both to you and to the defendant, with a note of the date and time of the hearing. The defendant is also sent a form (N.56), requiring information about his employment, pay and income, and liabilities, to complete and return to the court. If the defendant returns the form, a copy is sent to you by the court.

You do not have to attend the attachment of earnings hearing provided you write to the court asking the court to deal with the application in your absence. But if you have received a copy of form N.56 and can show that some of the information contained in it is incorrect, you should attend. If the net wages disclosed appear low, you can ask the court to send to the employer a request for a statement of the defendant's earnings on form N.338.

the hearing
In many cases, neither party appears. If the defendant has returned form N.56 and the information given is sufficient, the registrar will make an order there and then.

If there is no N.56, the court office may already have required the defendant's employer (this is why that question on the N.337 is so important) to supply details of the defendant's net and gross earnings over the past ten pay periods. This information will often be sufficient to enable the registrar to make an order; either party can apply to vary the order if they are unhappy with the amount.

If no information is available, the registrar will order that a notice of an adjourned hearing (form N.58) be issued and served personally on the defendant. This warns the defendant that he may be committed to prison if he fails to turn up. If the defendant then neither attends nor completes and returns the N.56 form, the judge will usually order the defendant's committal to prison for contempt of court. Alternatively, the judge can order the debtor to be arrested and brought before him. When he is brought to court, he is usually released if he then completes form N.56. Sending the defendant to prison does not solve the problem and the order is usually discharged if and when the defendant completes the form N.56 and returns it to the court.

the amount
When deciding how much to order the employer to deduct, the registrar will start by calculating what the defendant would be entitled to receive if he were on supplementary benefit. This is based on the scale used by the DHSS as representing the needs of the defendant and his family, the amount of his rent or mortgage repayment, the cost of getting to work. That figure is called the 'protected earnings rate' and is a figure below which the defendant's earnings may not be reduced through the attachment of earnings order.

Part of the difference between the defendant's net income and the protected earnings rate will be ordered to be deducted: this figure is the 'normal deduction rate'. What proportion of the difference will be deducted depends on the defendant's other liabilities. Other debts are taken into account and particular debts, such as maintenance or repayments of overdue tax, are likely to be given priority in the registrar's calculations.

An order showing the employee's protected earnings rate and the normal deduction rate is sent to both parties and to the defendant's employers. The employers will then have to deduct from each weekly or monthly pay packet the amount shown as the normal deduction rate until the debt is paid off.

If, however, at any time the effect of such a deduction would be to reduce the defendant's income below the protected earnings rate, the deduction made by the employer has to be limited to such a figure as will leave the defendant's net income at the protected earnings rate. This may happen, for example, where the defendant receives irregular overtime payment. If, for example, the protected earnings rate were £75 and the normal deduction rate £15, and the defendant's net pay for one particular week were only £85, only £10 would be deducted that week.

Where a defendant is employed by a small firm – particularly where he has only just started work – his employers may be reluctant to make the deductions and, rather than get involved in the necessary book-keeping, they might dismiss the employee – which is of no advantage to the plaintiff. The court has power to suspend the order and instruct the defendant to make payments direct to the court of a sum equal to the normal deduction rate, which the court will pass on to the plaintiff. If the defendant fails to keep up these payments, the plaintiff should contact the court and ask for the order to be 'directed' to the employer.

If the payer changes his job and you know the new employer, you can apply to the court for the order to be 'redirected'. If not, the order lapses.

garnishee order

The court can be asked to make an order requiring anybody who owes money to a debtor to pay this money into the court instead of to the person to whom they owe it. The court will pay the money out to the plaintiff. The most usual body to be garnisheed is the defendant's bank.

The procedure for a garnishee order is to complete and swear an affidavit using form N.349 and to send it together with the fee (£12) to the county court where judgment was obtained. The registrar then issues a garnishee order nisi.

If you are seeking a garnishee order against a bank, it is desirable, but not necessary, to give details of the defendant's branch and, if possible, account number. An order nisi freezes any of the defendant's money in the garnishee's hands at the date of service, until the full hearing of the garnishee application.

The order affects only money due at the date the garnishee order nisi is served on the garnishee. If the garnishee order nisi is served on the bank while the defendant's account is overdrawn – perhaps on the day before the defendant's pay cheque is paid in, the defendant then being overdrawn – the fact that he goes into credit the next day helps the plaintiff not at all. The bank can pay nothing because there was no money owing by them to the defendant at the time the order nisi was served on them.

Once the garnishee order nisi is served, the garnishee can either pay the money into court (the bank can deduct £30 for their own expenses) or can wait for the garnishee order absolute. In most cases, such money as is available is paid into court and notice given to the plaintiff. If the amount paid into court is the whole of the debt (subject to the £30 deduction), the plaintiff should ask for the money to be paid out to him.

If the bank pays only a part of the amount into court, the plaintiff has little option but to accept it in full settlement; otherwise, the bank will have to send someone to attend the hearing and the plaintiff may be ordered to pay the bank's legal costs if he is unable to prove that the bank owes the debtor more than they have paid into court.

Where no payment is made into court, the plaintiff has to attend court on the date fixed for the hearing to ask for the order to be made absolute, so that it can be enforced against the garnishee.

However, if the bank informs the court that there is no money in the defendant's account, the plaintiff should immediately ask the court for the garnishee proceedings to be withdrawn. Otherwise, the bank and the defendant may have a claim against the plaintiff for costs.

court fees

In all cases of enforcement, if the selected method is unsuccessful, the court fee paid by the plaintiff is lost and cannot be recovered from the defendant. If money is paid as a result of the order, the fee can be recovered by adding it to the judgment debt.

In the case of an execution against goods that has failed, if a subsequent warrant of execution is successful, both fees can be recovered.

charging order

Another method of enforcement is a charging order, which is a form of security. A charging order is usually made against land or a house owned by the defendant (even if owned jointly with, for example, a spouse). It can, however, also be made against stocks and shares, against money in court or other forms of security.

A charging order places the plaintiff in the same position as a mortgagee of land – that is, his debt will be paid out of the proceeds of selling the property (if there is sufficient left after any prior charges are discharged). But if he wants payment before the defendant chooses to sell the land or house, the plaintiff has to take separate court proceedings to enforce the sale.

A charging order against land owned by the defendant is first made as a charging order nisi. To obtain this, the plaintiff must file at court the plaint note and an affidavit which must

* give the name and address of the debtor and the amount owing
* if known, give the name of any other creditor who can be identified
* identify the subject matter of the charge
* verify the debtor's ownership of or interest in the asset.

The fee for applying for a charging order is £12.

The plaintiff is required to give the reasons for saying that he believes the defendant to own (jointly or solely) an interest in the land or house to be charged. When making an application for a charging order nisi by affidavit, you can apply to the court for an order giving you leave to inspect the Land Registry entry for the property which you believe to be owned by the defendant. This is one of the rare exceptions to the rule that no-one is entitled to inspect the register without the proprietor's permission.

Land Registry inspection
To find out which local land registry covers the area in which the defendant's property is situated, telephone the Land Registry in London (01-405 3488) or your nearest local land registry (listed in the telephone directory). The prescribed form of index map search (Land Registry form 96) is obtainable from HMSO and law stationery shops. You should complete and send it to the appropriate land registry. You will be told whether the property is registered and what the title number is. The registrar should be asked to make an order giving you leave to inspect the land register relating to that title.

You should then obtain from HMSO or a law stationery shop a form of request for office copy entries (Land Registry form A44) and send this to the land registry together with the court's order. In due course (about six weeks), you will get the official copies.

The charging order nisi itself imposes a charge on the property when registered at the land registry and secures you priority against other charges after the date you register it. Even if the defendant is made bankrupt, the charging order nisi gives you security provided it has been registered as a pending action.

the hearing
A date is fixed for a hearing to make the order absolute. You should attend this hearing. If the defendant also attends, the registrar will probably explain to him what the effect of the order is and then ask if he has any objections. In reality, very few objections would have any effect and the order is made more or less as a matter of course except where the defendant is a joint owner of the property.

Some courts require a wife to be served with notice of the hearing and, if the wife turns up, she may be able to establish an interest in the property, effectively reducing the husband-defendant's interest to nil, and argue that the charging order should not be made absolute. If you get warning of an application by a wife wanting to attend the hearing for the charging order absolute, you should get legal advice.

If the order absolute is made, it needs to be registered at the land registry.

unregistered land
If the land involved is not registered, there is no means of discovering by searches whether or not the defendant owns the property (although a search against the defendant's name at the Land Charges Registry might produce some evidence of ownership indirectly). The charging

orders nisi and absolute need to be registered as a charge against the property at the Land Charges Registry, Burrington Way, Plymouth PL5 3LP.

order for sale

Obtaining a charging order absolute does not, of itself, provide immediate payment of the debt, although the threat of an order for sale may well prompt the defendant to pay off the debt or at least make regular payments to reduce it. If not, and you do not wish to wait until the defendant voluntarily sells his house, you will have to obtain an order for sale. For this, you will need professional assistance.

Courts, however, are reluctant to order a sale unless the outstanding debt is large or the defendant is making no effort whatsoever to pay the debt. If, for example, you are owed £1,000 and the debtor is paying this off fairly regularly at the rate of £40 a month, and you have obtained a charging order, it would be unlikely that any order for sale would be made unless the defendant ceased payments for several months, leaving a substantial sum outstanding. Indeed, the court, on making the charging order absolute, might order it not to be enforced while the debtor pays the instalments ordered.

oral examination

It is possible to have any defendant who has a judgment order against him brought to court to be 'orally examined' on oath, by the registrar or a court officer. The purpose is to discover whether the defendant is employed and, if so, how and when he is paid, whether and where he has a bank account, whether money is owed to him, whether he owns a house or stocks and shares.

In the majority of cases, creditors simply issue a warrant of execution after judgment, knowing little or nothing about the debtor's circumstances, and then consider alternative methods of enforcement if the warrant is unsuccessful. An oral examination, after judgment but before any form of enforcement, is desirable for a warrant of execution and essential for all other methods. In cases where the debt is relatively small, the fees lost on a particular method of enforcement being unsuccessful can be significantly large. An oral examination which showed a bank deposit account but no real chattels of value would save the creditor from issuing a warrant of execution which proved abortive.

An oral examination takes place in the county court for the area where the defendant lives. If this is not the court in which you have obtained judgment, you must write to the court where you obtained judgment and ask for the action to be transferred to the defendant's court for the purposes of an oral examination.

To request an oral examination, you need to complete form N.316, and send it to the court with the fee of £12. The notice of the oral examination will be served on the defendant by the court. If the defendant is a limited company, one of the directors can be ordered to attend.

You will be told the date and time and should attend the hearing. Evidence is given on oath. If you do not attend, the registrar or court officer will ask the defendant questions and keep a record of his replies.

The court will discover many routine things from the defendant – whether he owns his home, if he has a car or other assets, where his bank account is, what is in it, what his main debts are, what he is paying monthly or weekly towards any court debts. You may feel that there are less routine questions that need to be put to the defendant, particularly if you have knowledge of specific facts that might help in getting a fuller picture. You are entitled to cross-examine the defendant as severely as you wish, with a view to obtaining any relevant information. You must do your homework and prepare a list of questions you want him to answer: you will not get an opportunity like this again.

In some county courts, pro forma questions are used at oral examinations, and the creditor is discouraged from asking additional questions. This should be resisted most strongly.

If the defendant does not attend, you can ask the court to fix a date for an adjourned hearing before the judge. You have to pay the fee (£5) and 'conduct money' (likely expenses for the defendant to attend the hearing). If the defendant does not attend this hearing, the judge will make an order committing the defendant to prison. But he will not be sent to prison if at the last moment he attends at the court and gives evidence as to his means and assets.

a builder's claim for payment

Bill Kevins, a jobbing builder, was called in by Jane Robinson to build a small patio for her house. She asked him for an estimate and he wrote to her with details of the work he was to do for a price of £350 plus VAT. Jane accepted, and arranged for Bill to start work. He was a few days late in starting but that did not worry Jane.

While Bill was clearing the site and digging down to enable him to lay a base for the patio, Jane decided that instead of the concrete slabs she originally asked Bill to lay, she would like Ebor stone slabs. She asked Bill to obtain some and Bill agreed – but nothing was said about any difference in the price already estimated. While Bill was finishing off the patio, Jane asked him to repair the garden gate and to replace some guttering; again, nothing was said about price.

When all was finished, Bill asked Jane to sign a note which he had prepared confirming that the work had been carried out to her satisfaction. A few days later, Jane received the bill which was for a total of £700 plus VAT. Jane wrote to tell Bill that she thought that this was excessive, that she expected him to stick to the £350 estimate for the patio but was prepared to pay a further £80 plus VAT for the extra work to the gate and gutter. She sent him a cheque for £494.50. The next day, it rained heavily and sand started being washed away from under the paving slabs; by the following morning, they were looking very uneven.

Alarmed by this, Jane stopped the cheque and wrote to Bill asking him to come back and put the patio right, saying that she would not pay him until this was done. Bill did not answer directly but a few days later a solicitor's letter arrived, notifying Jane that the cheque had been dishonoured and warning her that unless payment was made in full in 14 days, Bill would commence court proceedings. Jane replied to the solicitor saying that she had never agreed to pay £700 plus VAT, that the price was excessive and that the work was not done properly. She said that she would pay nothing until Bill came back and put the patio right.

Nothing happened for several weeks and then Bill himself started proceedings in the local county court. (He had decided that he would not instruct solicitors.)

His particulars of claim read as follows:

IN THE ANYTOWN COUNTY COURT   Case No. 85.01123
BETWEEN
                    WILLIAM KEVINS   plaintiff
                    and
                    JANE ROBINSON   defendant

PARTICULARS OF CLAIM

1.   The plaintiff is a builder and the defendant is the owner of 123 Elm Avenue, Anytown.

2.   In February 1985, the plaintiff agreed with the defendant to carry out works for the construction of a patio for the defendant, at a price of £350 plus VAT. In the course of carrying out such works, the agreement was varied by the parties by the substitution of Ebor stone paving slabs for concrete slabs, no price for such variation being agreed. It was further agreed that the plaintiff would repair a gate and replace guttering to the rear of the defendant's house, no price being agreed for such work.

3.   The additional cost of the provision of Ebor stone paving slabs amounted to £100 plus VAT and the cost of repairing the gate and replacing guttering (materials and labour) amounted to £250 plus VAT.

4.   On 12th March 1985, the plaintiff invoiced the defendant for £805 (£700 plus VAT).

5.   On 28th March 1985, the defendant sent the plaintiff a cheque for £494.50. This cheque was dishonoured on presentation. Notice of dishonour was given on 9th April 1985 by Messrs. White and Brown, the plaintiff's solicitors, telling her that the cheque had been dishonoured by the bank. The cheque has not been met on re-presentation .

And the plaintiff claims:

(a) payment of the sum of £494.50 due on the dishonoured cheque

(b) payment of the balance of the plaintiff's bill, namely £310.50

(c) interest at 15% per annum from 28th March 1985 to the date of this claim, namely £13.23 and thereafter until judgment at a daily rate of 33p.

(d) costs.

Dated this 7th day of May 1985

                              Signed: *William Kevins*
                              who will accept service
                              of any proceedings at
                              42 Firs Lane, Anytown.

Jane straightaway completed the form of 'admission, defence and counterclaim' saying:

1.   The defendant admits paragraphs 1, 2 & 4 of the particulars of claim but says that there was an implied agreement between the parties that the Ebor paving slabs were to be provided by the plaintiff at no additional cost to the defendant.

2.   As to paragraph 3, the defendant says that a fair and reasonable price for the repair to the gate and the replacement of guttering would be £80 plus VAT.

3.   As to paragraph 5, the defendant admits that she instructed her bank not to honour the cheque for £494.50.

4.   The plaintiff failed properly to construct the patio, in breach of the agreement between the plaintiff and the defendant that the plaintiff would carry out the work with reasonable skill.

5.   Within two weeks of the construction of the patio, the sand on which the paving slabs were set was washed away by rain, leaving an uneven and dangerous surface. The plaintiff has refused to remedy the defects.

6.   The cost of remedying the defects will amount to £240 plus VAT.

And the defendant counterclaims:

1.   Payment of £240 plus VAT and interest on this at 15% per annum from the date on which the work is carried out until judgment.

2.   Costs

Date: 14 May 1985   Signed: *Jane Robinson*

                                               whose address for service
                                               is 123 Elm Avenue, Anytown.

The pleadings set out the basic facts and make clear the points at issue between the two of them. If lawyers were involved, there might well be a request for further and better particulars of both claim and counterclaim.

   The registrar decides that this would be a case in which a preliminary hearing would be of value, so a date is fixed for this.

   At the preliminary hearing, Bill says that as he was given a cheque, he should have judgment for the amount of the cheque. Jane objects, saying that the work was defective and there should be no payment until the whole dispute is resolved. It is a principle of law that where payment is made by cheque, the plaintiff should not be put in a worse position than if cash had been paid. The registrar decides that the plaintiff is entitled to part judgment of £494.50, to be paid within 14 days, and orders that the balance of the claim should be referred to arbitration.

He next considers the question of documents. The main documents were the estimates, bills and letters passing between Bill and Jane. In addition, there were receipts for materials bought by Bill. The registrar orders that the plaintiff prepare a bundle of all the documents passing between the parties, together with the receipts for materials, with a copy to the defendant and a copy to the court. (This is simpler than preparing a formal list of documents.)

Next comes the question of expert evidence. Bill says that he does not intend to call any. The registrar advises him that it would be wise for him to get some outside evidence as to the method of construction of the patio and the additional cost of the paving slabs and of the work to the gate and the guttering. Jane says that she has already arranged for a chartered surveyor to inspect the work. The registrar directs that each expert report be disclosed to the other side within 28 days and agreed if possible. (No expert evidence would be allowed at the hearing except from experts whose reports have been so disclosed.)

The registrar then directs that the arbitration be fixed on the first open (that is, available) day after 6 weeks. He estimates that the hearing would last two hours.

Bill prepares the bundle of documents as directed but decides that he would not go to the expense of obtaining an expert's report; he feels that his 20 years of experience as a builder made him as much of an 'expert' as any surveyor.

The local surveyor who had been instructed by Jane to inspect the work produces a report saying that the patio was not constructed properly and that the slabs should have been placed on a sand and cement mix which would not have been damaged by rain. He places the cost of putting this right at £200 plus VAT. He says that the Ebor stone paving slabs would have cost between £80 and £100 more than concrete slabs. He advises that the reasonable cost of repairing the gate would have been £40 and of replacing the guttering £100.

Jane sends a copy of the report to Bill asking him if he would agree the contents. She also says that she would increase her offer to settle to

	£	
Original bill	350	
plus	90	cost of Ebor paving
plus	40	repairing gate
plus	100	guttering
	580	
+ VAT	87	
	667	

less £200		cost of remedial work
+ VAT 30	230	
	£437	

As there is already a part judgment for £494.50 in Bill's favour, she needs a judgment on the counterclaim for £57.50 to reduce the payment due to Bill to what she considers the correct amount of £437.

She stresses that this is an 'open' offer which she would draw to the attention of the registrar after the hearing. Had she offered more than the amount of the existing judgment, she would have been wise, even in an arbitration, to pay the excess into court and give notice to the plaintiff, but as she maintains that the existing judgment is for too much, she cannot do this; the open offer in her letter serves the same purpose.

Bill is getting fed up with the whole business but is not inclined to settle on the basis that Jane has suggested. He writes back and says that he will settle for £494.50 plus his court fee plus the solicitor's costs incurred at the start of bringing proceedings (£25 plus VAT), plus a further £100. Jane will not agree to this, particularly as solicitors' costs are not normally recoverable in this way, and so the case goes to the arbitration hearing.

At that hearing, Bill, as plaintiff, first gives evidence about the way he carried out the work. He produces all the correspondence and the receipt for the Ebor stone slabs. He says that it was never agreed and he never would have agreed, that the extra cost of Ebor stone slabs would be borne by him. He cannot produce evidence as to the cost of the concrete slabs but says that he would accept the higher of the surveyor's figures – £100 – as the difference. He says that the gate needed 8 hours to repair at £8 per hour and that materials cost £12. The guttering cost £40 for materials and 12 hours' work.

The registrar asks Jane if she wants to question Bill. Jane decides not to, but to rely on her expert's evidence.

The registrar then asks the defendant, Jane, to tell him about the agreement for the work to be done and about the change in plans with regard to paving materials. Jane agrees that nothing had been said about any increase in cost either by Bill or by her. She says that as Bill did not warn her about any increased cost, she should not have to pay it.

She describes how the patio had become uneven as a result of the first heavy rainfall after laying. She says that she did not believe that Bill had spent as much time as 8 hours on the gate and that the guttering had been done in just over a day.

The surveyor called by Jane then gives evidence. He produces his report and answers the registrar's questions. Essentially, he says that the way in which Bill had constructed the patio was not good building practice and that the slabs would have to be taken up and a proper base constructed. He says that in his view, this would cost £200. He thought that 5 hours would have been more than enough to repair the gate and that it should not have needed more than 6 hours to take down the old guttering and replace it. He agreed with Bill's materials costs.

The registrar asks Bill if he wants to ask the surveyor questions. Bill, in fact, just repeats his own evidence about the time taken. The registrar asks him if he had any time sheets or other records of time spent but Bill has none.

The registrar then asks Bill if there was anything else he wanted to say and then puts the same question to Jane. Neither wants to add anything.

The registrar then gives judgment. He says that he had a number of questions to decide. First, was there an implied agreement that Bill would supply Ebor paving slabs at the same cost as concrete slabs and, if not, what was the additional cost? Secondly, what was the reasonable cost of labour and materials for the gate and guttering? Thirdly, had the patio been constructed properly and, if not, what was the reasonable cost of putting it right?

As to the first question, the registrar says that although it was unfortunate that nothing was said about increased cost, the substitution of Ebor stone paving slabs was a clear alteration in the terms of the original agreement between Bill and Jane. Jane must pay the extra cost. Bill had not produced any evidence as to the cost of the slabs that he had originally intended to supply and the registrar found that £90 – the middle point of the surveyor's figures – was a reasonable extra charge. As to the gate, the registrar felt that Bill had been overcharging for the extra work. He accepted the charge of £8 per hour as reasonable but decided that, at most, five hours' work was required. Likewise, he accepted that six hours was a reasonable time for the guttering work.

The registrar says that he accepted the surveyor's evidence as to the construction of the patio and his estimate of the cost of putting it right.

The registrar decides that Bill is entitled to be paid:

	£
original estimate	350
extra cost of paving stones	90
labour cost for gate	40
material cost for gate	12
labour cost for gutter	48
material cost for gutter	40
	580
add VAT	87
	£667

From this, he deducts £230, being the estimated cost of the repair work, including VAT. This leaves £437 due to Bill. As there is already a part judgment for £494.50 to be paid to Bill, this means that he allows Jane her counterclaim for £57.50. (Alternatively the registrar could have made an order for Bill to be paid £172.50 (i.e. £667 minus the £494.50 already ordered) and an order for Jane to be paid £230 – the net effect would be the same.)

Both sides then claim costs. Bill says that he had had to come to court to get payment and Jane produces a copy of her letter with the offer of the same figure as the registrar's (albeit on a slightly different basis) pointing out that Bill had refused to settle on this basis.

The registrar decides that Jane should pay Bill the court fee for issuing the summons, and that Bill should pay Jane the fee for the expert's report and for the expert's attendance to give evidence, and also her loss of wages for attending the arbitration.

possession cases

Where somebody wants to enforce a right to reclaim a property in which someone else is living, a court order is needed. The three common forms of possession cases in which a householder may become involved are

* mortgage possession
* claims for possession of rented property
* claims for possession of property against a person who has no legal right of occupation – squatters' cases.

mortgage possession cases

When money is borrowed from a building society, bank or finance house, security is usually given in the form of a legal charge on the borrower's home. The owner of the house, in return for the loan, agrees to make repayment of that loan either on demand or, more usually, by regular instalments of capital and interest or of interest only with collateral security in the form of an endowment insurance policy, designed to pay off the loan on its maturity. If the borrower fails to make the required payments, the lender has the right to take possession of the house. The legal charge sets out the circumstances – usually, failure to repay the money on being given notice to do so, or failure to pay a specified number of repayments.

In general, lenders are not anxious to take court proceedings for possession, and often allow a certain amount of leeway to borrowers who fall behind with their payments.

If the arrears have built up to such an extent, however, that the lender feels it necessary to start proceedings, these will normally be taken in the county court for the area in which the property is situated. A summons is served on the borrower together with a copy of the particulars of claim. It is a fixed-date summons for a hearing by a registrar in chambers. If you get such a summons, consult a CAB or housing advice centre straightaway.

With the summons comes a standard form to complete and return to the court, indicating whether or not you agree with the arrears of repayments as stated in the particulars of claim. You can make any offer you feel able to, to repay these arrears.

It is sensible to approach the lender with any proposals you have to make about paying off the arrears or selling the property before any hearing. The lender may be prepared to ask for the hearing to be adjourned on the terms agreed between you (but you may have to pay the costs of the lender's solicitor attending court).

The court has power to adjourn the hearing of an application for possession of a mortgaged dwellinghouse if it is satisfied that the outstanding amount can be repaid within a reasonable period.

The 'amount outstanding' is the total amount of any monthly repayments in arrear – usually a relatively small sum compared with the total amount of the debt. If £10,000 were borrowed from a bank under a house loan scheme and the bank agreed to accept repayments by instalments of, say, £100 per month and you had failed to make the last six payments, the court would be concerned to establish that you could pay the normal repayments and in addition pay off the £600 arrears over a reasonable period.

What is a reasonable period for repayment of the money outstanding depends on the circumstances. A realistic proposal to pay off the arrears within one year should be acceptable. A longer period may be acceptable to the court, but the longer the period, the more the court will need to be certain that the payments can be kept up.

hearing of the application

At the hearing, a representative of the plaintiff (the bank or building society) has to produce the charge certificate and an affidavit confirming that the contents of the particulars of claim are true, and giving up-to-date particulars of the arrears. You should have been supplied with a copy of the affidavit in advance.

The registrar will probably ask you if you agree the amount of the arrears as stated in the affidavit. If not, you should say what you believe the arrears to be and why you think the figure in the affidavit is wrong. For example, you might have made a recent payment which has not been taken into account; if so, you should produce a receipt for this payment. If the registrar cannot establish the correct amount of the arrears, he may adjourn the hearing for further evidence – asking perhaps for a list of all payments that the lender says that you have made over the past year or so, for you to check these.

When the amount of the arrears can be agreed, the registrar will want to know what proposals you have for discharging them. It is important to make definite proposals and also to be able to satisfy the registrar that you can keep up these payments together with the normal repayments. You should bring your last 3 payslips to court for this reason, and any other documents that may be helpful in showing that you can pay.

The registrar can either adjourn the case for the arrears to be paid off or he can make a suspended order – that is, an order for possession that cannot be enforced unless you do not pay off the arrears at the rate stated in the order. Once the arrears are paid off, the order ceases to have effect. For example, if there were arrears of £1,000 and you could manage to pay £100 a month in addition to the normal repayment, the registrar might order "Possession in 28 days, suspended on payment of arrears of £1,000 by monthly instalments of £100 in addition to current repayments."

enforcement

If your circumstances are such that you have no chance whatsoever of paying off the arrears, there may well be no alternative to selling the house. The registrar then normally makes an order for possession in 28 days which means that, once the 28 days are up, the lender is entitled to instruct the court bailiff to take possession of the house.

It may be that you would prefer to deal with the sale of the house yourself: you are likely to get a better price if the house is sold by you and you can show prospective purchasers round a furnished and occupied home. If you request this, the registrar may be prepared to give you some time to do so. You should contact estate agents as soon as possible – preferably before the hearing – and get a valuation and instruct them to place the house on the market. Ask them for a letter to produce to the registrar showing that they have got the house on the market and that it is being offered at a realistic price. The registrar may still make an order for possession, but he may well give a substantially longer period – say, up to three months.

suspending the order

At any stage before a warrant of possession is actually executed – that is, the bailiff takes possession for the lender – you have the right to apply to the court

* to extend the period for giving possession
* to vary the terms under which the order for possession is suspended
* to suspend an order which has not previously been suspended.

Thus, if at the time of the hearing you felt there was no chance of paying off the arrears and an order for possession in 28 days was given but you then unexpectedly obtained work, you could apply for the order to be suspended.

An application to extend, vary or suspend should be made on form N.244, and should state clearly what sort of order you are seeking – for example, "that the order for possession made on the 1st July 1985 be suspended on payment of the arrears by monthly instalments of £100". The application should be taken or sent to the court office. A date and time for a hearing will be inserted and you should send a copy of the application to the lender's solicitors.

You should take to the hearing any documentary evidence you have to support your application – for example, letter from estate agents or solicitor with regard to possible sale, evidence of your income from employment, and suchlike.

costs

In mortgage possession proceedings, you will almost certainly be liable to pay the lender's costs, under the terms of your mortgage agreement. The costs can be quite substantial and for this reason alone it is important to avoid unnecessary adjournments and applications to the court.

If a suspended order for possession is made, ask the building society or other lender to let you have a copy of their solicitor's bill of costs as soon as they receive it. This has two advantages. The costs are usually "added to the security", but if you are able to pay the costs straightaway or by instalments, you will avoid the amount of the costs being added to the capital outstanding and thus attracting interest and putting off the day when the mortgage will be paid off. Also, it gives you the opportunity, as the ultimate payer of the bill, to apply for taxation of the bill – this means that the court taxing officer checks that the amount of the bill is reasonable. Your local citizens advice bureau will be able to tell you how to get this done if the lender's solicitor will not help, but ask him first.

rented property

Where a house, flat or room is let as a dwellinghouse, a landlord seeking possession – and any occupier against whom possession is claimed – needs to know whether the tenancy is one that is protected by the Rent Act 1977 or the Housing Act 1980, in which case he cannot take possession without having obtained a court order.

The Housing Act in general gives protection to tenants of local housing authorities and also tenants of most housing associations. Most other private tenancies and some private licences are protected to a varying extent by the Rent Act.

The law relating to landlord and tenant is complicated. If you are unclear about your own position, you should seek expert advice – for instance, through a citizens advice bureau. For tenants in the London area, SHAC, an independent housing aid centre, can give advice and help on individual problems: telephone 373 7276. There are a number of SHAC publications, including a booklet *Private tenants: protection from eviction* (60p) and *The Housing Rights Guide* (£4.95), available from SHAC, 189a Old Brompton Road, London SW5 0AR. The Consumer Publication *Renting and letting* (£5.95) deals with the subject of security of tenure in some detail.

protected by the Rent Act?

The Rent Act 1977 gives full protection to the tenancy of any dwelling – even a single room – whether or not furnished, which is let as a separate dwelling. There has to be a tenancy: with an agreement described as a 'licence', the occupier may not be fully protected under the Rent Act.

Certain tenancies do not come within this protection, including

• a letting where the landlord is a government department, a local authority or a housing association (but local authority and housing association tenancies are generally secure tenancies under the Housing Act 1980)

• where the letting is a genuine holiday letting

• where the dwelling is let as part of a business letting (such as a flat over a shop where both flat and shop are let under the same agreement)

• a tenant sharing living accommodation with the landlord (sharing with another tenant does not necessarily prevent the Rent Act applying).

An important protection under the Rent Act is that even if the tenancy expires or is brought to an end by serving a 'notice to quit', the tenant remains protected by what is known as a statutory tenancy until that is brought to an end by a court order.

Where the letting is fully protected by the Rent Act, the landlord has to prove that the original contractual tenancy has been brought to an end because it was for a fixed period which has run out, or by serving a valid notice to quit, and also that one of the statutory grounds for possession (set out in Schedule 15 to the Rent Act 1977) has been satisfied.

cases when landlord can get possession

The statutory grounds for possession are called 'cases'. Those in Part I of Schedule 15 are discretionary – that is, the court has to consider whether or not it is reasonable to make an order for possession. They are

* rent arrears
* breach of any obligation of the tenancy
* nuisance or annoyance to adjoining occupiers
* conviction of tenant for using premises for illegal or immoral purposes
* deterioration of condition of the dwellinghouse or furniture let with it because of wilful conduct or neglect
* tenant revoking own notice to quit when landlord has contracted to sell or re-let
* tenant assigning or subletting in breach of tenancy agreement
* in a service tenancy, where tenant no longer employee of landlord
* landlord reasonably requiring property as a home for himself or immediate family
* tenant has sublet and is overcharging rent.

In these cases, the court must not only be satisfied that the ground for possession exists and that the tenancy has been validly terminated but also that it is reasonable to make the order. The court may also make an order for possession at its discretion (without the landlord having to prove any of the cases) if it is satisfied that suitable alternative accommodation is available to the tenant, or will be available to him when the order for possession takes effect.

In the other cases (Part II of the Schedule), the court **must** make an order for possession provided it is satisfied that the tenancy has been validly terminated or come to an end and that the ground for possession is proved. They are

* owner wanting to re-occupy property after temporary letting
* owner wanting to occupy property as his home on retirement
* letting of a holiday home out of season
* letting of student accommodation outside term time
* temporary letting of accommodation normally used as a residence for clergyman, for farm worker or farm manager
* a protected shorthold tenancy
* member of armed forces now requiring property for his occupation.

Whatever the grounds for seeking possession, it is essential that the contractual tenancy has been validly terminated by the landlord before the date that court proceedings are started. If proceedings are commenced before the tenancy has been terminated, they are bound to be dismissed.

giving notice to quit

A notice to quit must be for at least 28 days, more if the original tenancy agreement required a longer notice. It must terminate on either the anniversary of the commencement of the tenancy – that is, the same day of the week (if a weekly tenancy) or the same day of the month (if a monthly tenancy) – or on the day when rent is due to be paid. This is important: the notice must expire on the appropriate date. If the landlord generously gave six months' notice but expressed it so as to expire on the wrong day, he would have to start all over again and give notice to expire on a correct day.

The notice to quit must contain a notice in statutory form telling the tenant that he has the right to remain in the property until a court makes an order for possession.

The form of the notice to quit is important, so one of the printed forms obtainable from law stationery shops should be used; a copy may be available from a citizens advice bureau or from a housing advice centre.

Since the court will have to be satisfied, on a reasonable balance of probabilities, that the notice to quit has come to the personal attention of the tenant, send it by recorded delivery with 'advice of receipt' service. Or serve the notice to quit personally on the tenant or his wife (or one of the tenants if there are more than one), and ask the tenant to acknowledge receipt by signing a form of receipt endorsed on a copy of the notice to quit.

landlord taking proceedings

The landlord must wait until the notice to quit has expired before commencing court proceedings. Most county courts have available forms of particulars of claim for litigants in person, suitable in simple cases of rent arrears or where the landlord is a resident landlord. In other cases, it would be sensible for the landlord to get legal help in drafting the particulars of claim.

Once the notice to quit has (safely) expired, the summons can be issued in the same way as any other summons: take two copies of the particulars of claim to the court office with the fee and with a request for issue of a summons (form N.204 request for summons for recovery of land). Remember to keep a copy of the particulars of claim for yourself.

With a summons for possession, a date is given straightaway for the hearing of the action in open court, usually in four to six weeks' time.

Before the hearing, the landlord should get all the necessary documents together. In most cases, these will be the following.

• Evidence of title to the property. It will be sufficient to produce a written tenancy agreement. But if there is none, evidence of title must be produced.

If the property is registered, the best evidence is to produce the land certificate or, if there is a mortgage on the property, copy entries from the land registry where the house is registered. If you know the title number, you can apply to the land registry on form A.44 for office copies. If you do not know the title number, you can apply to the land registry for an 'index map search' on form 96 and send this with form 99 leaving the space for the title number blank. These forms are all available from law stationers.

If the property is unregistered, the title deeds will have to be produced. If there is a mortgage on the property and the lender is not prepared to release the title deeds to you, you may have to instruct a solicitor because the lender will probably only be prepared to release the deeds to him. Or you may have to issue a witness summons to require an officer of the lender to attend court with the deeds.

• Copy of the tenancy agreement, if there is one.

• Copy of the notice to quit – preferably with the tenant's receipt of service endorsed or a copy of your covering letter and the signed recorded delivery advice card.

● A record of rent payments – and non-payments – if you are relying on failure to pay rent as the ground for possession. Have three copies: one for the court, one for the tenant (defendant) and one to keep yourself.

If you are relying on any copy documents where the original is in the hands of the tenant, it is important to serve a 'notice to admit' (form N.283) on the tenant so that he may inspect the copy, and if necessary object to it as not corresponding to the original. If he does not object, the copy is admissible at the hearing, subject to your also serving (at the same time) a 'notice to produce' the original at the hearing (form N.284).

settlement before the hearing

You may be approached by your tenant or his legal adviser with suggestions for settling the action. The tenant may say, for example, that he would not oppose an order for possession if you waived any claim for the arrears of rent. Or the suggestion may be for a suspended order – that is, an order for possession suspended so long as the tenant pays off the arrears of rent at certain weekly or monthly amounts in addition to the normal rent payments.

In all cases where the court has a discretion whether or not to grant an order for possession, the judge has the final word as to whether any arrangement you make will be incorporated into a court order. He must be satisfied that the proposed terms are reasonable before making them into an order.

If the proposed settlement is that the tenant will let you have possession if you waive the arrears of rent, you need to weigh up the amount of the arrears you will forgo against any problem you might have in getting an order for possession. If the arrears are large, you may consider that you would be better off getting a new tenant who might be a more reliable payer.

If the tenant wants to stay in the property, you have to consider whether the offer to pay off the arrears is reasonable, having regard to the tenant's means. If not, it may be better to take your chance with the court.

In any case, it will make things easier if you can agree how much rent is owing, to get any disputes about the amount of the arrears out of the way before the hearing.

tenant defending a claim for possession

If you as tenant receive a summons, look carefully at the particulars of claim to see if it includes a clause such as "the plaintiff claims possession pursuant to Case .. of Schedule 15 to the Rent Act 1977". That makes clear that the landlord accepts that you have protection under the Rent Act. If such a clause is not included, you can assume that the landlord claims that you are not entitled to protection under the Rent Act. This is an extremely important point and you should seek advice from a solicitor, local housing advice centre or CAB to find out whether or not you are entitled to such protection.

If possession is claimed under the Rent Act 1977, citing a particular case under Schedule 15, you should check whether the 'case' is a discretionary one (where the court must be satisfied that it is reasonable to make the order for possession: cases 1 to 10) or a mandatory one (where the court must make the order, provided it is satisfied that the tenancy has been terminated and the specific ground for possession proved: cases 11 to 20).

If the claim for possession is on one of the latter grounds (when the court must make an order), the only defence that is possible is

- that the tenancy has not been validly terminated, and/or
- that the facts on which the landlord's case relies do not satisfy the requirements of the particular 'case'.

example of a Part II claim

Where at the date the tenancy was granted, the landlord occupied the house as his own dwelling and gave written notice to the tenant that possession might be recovered on the basis that he was originally an owner occupier, he can base his claim on case 11.

The landlord will have to prove that he was an owner occupier at the time this tenancy (or any immediately preceding tenancies) was granted. He also has to prove that, when granting the tenancy, he gave notice in writing that he would wish to resume possession in due course when requiring the house for his own residence (or that of a member of his family who lived with him when he last occupied the house as a residence). The landlord must have served a notice to quit terminating the tenancy on an appropriate date and including the statutory formula as to the right of the tenant to remain in occupation until a court has made an order for possession.

Provided the landlord gives evidence of his intention to resume residence, the court will not enquire into the reasonableness of the landlord's intention. It is, therefore, difficult to challenge the landlord unless he claims, for example, to want to occupy the property himself but you know that he has another posting abroad commencing immediately after the termination of his present contract.

If you are able to dispute any of the facts that the landlord has to prove, you should complete the form of defence sent to you with the particulars of claim, making it clear what parts of the particulars of claim you dispute and, in outline, the facts which you rely on to dispute them.

You will need to get your evidence together and arrange for witnesses to attend court.

example of a Part I claim

Where there are rent arrears, or you are accused of creating a nuisance, or the landlord wishes to recover possession to occupy the premises himself (not having given a 'case 11 notice'), the court has a discretion and you can try to argue that it would not be reasonable for the court to make the order for possession.

claim based on case 2: nuisance

Where the ground for seeking possession is that a nuisance is being caused – either to the landlord or to adjoining occupiers – details of the alleged nuisance should have been given in the landlord's particulars of claim. If not, you should ask for detailed particulars by letter. If these are not supplied within a reasonable time, apply to the court (on form N.244) for an order that such particulars be supplied.

The nuisance alleged might be continual playing of a radio or stereo late at night, noise from a dog, allowing refuse bins to remain uncleared,

or any one of 101 other things. You will need to see what evidence you can gather to dispute the alleged nuisance. If the allegation is broadly correct, the most sensible thing to do is to admit the allegation but propose ways of reducing the nuisance – for instance, undertaking to the court not to play radio or stereo after 11 pm.

If the nuisance alleged is not all that serious, the judge would probably be prepared to adjourn the case on your undertaking to put matters right, or possibly to make an order for possession suspended so long as you comply with the undertaking. He will certainly want to know why you did not put the matter right when the landlord complained.

claim based on case 1: rent arrears

Where the tenancy has been validly terminated and the landlord is claiming on the ground of rent arrears, you need to check

★ is the amount of arrears claimed correct?
★ is the periodic rent claimed legally recoverable?
★ are the calculations correct?
★ have all payments made by you been credited?
★ have you applied a 'rent stop' to offset repairs?

The weekly or monthly rent claimed may not be legally recoverable rent if, for example, there has been a rent increase and the landlord has not followed the proper 'fair rent' procedure, or if the rent agreed between the landlord and a new tenant at the beginning of the tenancy is higher than a previously registered 'fair rent'.

The next step is to check that the calculation of the rent arrears is correct. If there is a rent book, this should be relatively easy. If no rent book, ask the plaintiff landlord to produce a statement showing how the amount of the arrears is calculated (if necessary, applying to the court on form N.244 for an order that he do so).

preparing for hearing
All documents showing payments of rent made – receipts, rent books, letters, paid cheques etc. – should be got together in preparing for the hearing. If you dispute that the rent is legally recoverable, obtain copies of any rent registration from the rent officer. It is advisable to send copies of all documents to the plaintiff.

The judge's concern will be to decide what the arrears are, why they have occurred and how quickly they can be paid off. It is sensible to tell the judge the reason for the arrears – a period of unemployment or short-time working, or whatever it may be. If the rent can be paid off within a reasonable period in weekly or monthly instalments (in addition to current rent), the judge will probably make a suspended order for possession.

Where you have withheld rent because the landlord has failed to carry out his repairing obligations, you should seek legal advice about the possibility of getting an order requiring the landlord to carry out the repairs before the hearing. At the hearing, you should tell the judge that you are being advised, and ask for an adjournment if necessary.

If you are unemployed or on a low income, you may be entitled to housing benefit. If you have not applied for this, you should do so at once, to your local authority. A CAB or welfare rights worker can work out how much rebate you will get and this will help in working out how much of the arrears you can pay off. You may have applied for a rebate earlier but, because of a backlog of work, the housing benefit office has not processed it yet. You should tell the judge exactly when you applied and how much rebate it is estimated you will get. Some of the arrears may then be settled because benefit is backdated to the date of application.

the hearing

If you have reached a settlement, you should tell the judge about this as soon as your case is called. He may only want to hear confirmation from the tenant that the terms are agreed and then make an order in the agreed terms. Probably, however, he will wish to hear evidence as if the case were contested, because he is required under the Rent Act to exercise his discretion and may feel he cannot properly do so without hearing evidence.

If it is only the amount of the arrears that have been agreed, tell this to the judge at the outset.

The plaintiff might, for example, say "I am the landlord, your honour, I appear in person. The tenant is represented by his solicitor. We have been able to agree that the rent arrears to date amount to £. . . .".

He then goes into the witness box. Evidence is given on oath but you can affirm if you wish to. The evidence required to be given in the case of rent arrears is broadly as follows:

"My name is . . . .
"I live at . . . .
"I own the first floor flat at Willow Lane, Anytown.
"I produce the land certificate.

"I granted a tenancy of the flat to the defendant on 1 July 1983. There was no written agreement. The rent agreed was £35 per week.

"The defendant is now in arrear with the rent to the extent of £350. He has paid rent only on odd occasions over the last three months. I wrote to him asking him to pay rent regularly in future – here is a copy of the letter – but this made no difference.

"I therefore served on the defendant a notice to quit on 1 March 1985 by handing it to him. This notice expired on 30 April which was a day when rent was due to be paid. I produce a copy of the notice to quit.

"I ask for an order for possession of the flat."

The judge may well want to ask some questions. In particular, if the arrears of rent had not been agreed, he would want to see records of rent payments and ask the landlord questions about the system of recording rent payments.

If the defendant is opposing an order for possession, the judge will ask the defendant or his solicitor if they wish to question the plaintiff and, if so, he must answer any questions which are relevant. Sometimes in possession actions, tenants (or landlords) ask questions about matters which are not really relevant; if so, you can always ask the judge whether you have to answer the particular question and say why you think it is irrelevant.

Next, the defendant can give evidence. If he is not disputing the amount of the rent arrears, he may not wish to do so. But if the landlord is opposing an offer to pay by instalments which he feels are less than the tenant can afford, he can insist on the tenant taking the oath (or affirming) so that he can be questioned about his means.

You as landlord should ask him to produce payslips or other evidence of his income, and ask about any other sources of income – such as child benefit, part-time working, pensions, allowances etc. You will also need to discover what financial commitments he has, under court orders or HP agreements or suchlike. At the end, you will have an opportunity to argue that the tenant should be able to make a larger offer.

The defendant (tenant) can make any further comments to the judge before the plaintiff (landlord) closes his case; the plaintiff has the last word.

The judge then sums up and gives his decision.

If the judge makes a suspended order, the landlord should ask the judge to incorporate in the order a money judgment for the arrears. If the tenant then does not keep up payments and the landlord issues a warrant for possession, this enables him to seek payment of the arrears by the same warrant. The landlord is also entitled to ask the judge to make an order that the tenant pays the court fee and any witness fee – these being added on to the arrears of rent to be paid at the rate ordered by the judge.

An order for possession is generally made to take effect in 28 days' time; the court may allow longer where it is impractical for the tenant to find alternative accommodation within that period.

squatters

Squatters in vacant properties have neither tenancies nor generally the landlord's permission to occupy. County court rules provide a relatively quick procedure for obtaining possession where any person occupies land without the licence or consent of the owner or of any previous owner. This applies also where the occupier is there under the terms of a licence which has since been terminated.

The procedure to obtain an order for possession is for the plaintiff to file an originating application (using form N.312), together with an affidavit stating

* his interest in the land
* the circumstances under which the land has been occupied without his licence or consent and in which his claim to possession arises
* that he does not know the names of any occupier of the land other than stated in the originating application.

The plaintiff should lodge the affidavit and originating application at the court, together with copies of each for each named occupier. The fee payable is £20.

The court will fix a date for a hearing. A copy of the originating application and affidavit is served by the court on each named occupier. A copy will also be fixed to the door of the property, and a copy addressed to 'the occupiers' posted through the letterbox.

At the hearing, if the defendants – or any of them – can show that they had permission to occupy the premises and that permission has not been lawfully revoked, the judge or registrar will probably adjourn the case to enable fuller evidence to be given by both sides. He may direct that the originating application stand as a particulars of claim and that the action be treated as an ordinary fixed-date case.

In the most cases, however, an order is made for possession forthwith.

enforcement of an order for possession

Once the date for giving possession has passed, and the tenant is still there, an order for possession can be enforced by issuing a warrant for possession.

In order to issue a warrant for possession, the plaintiff has to send or take to the court

* form of request (N.325)
* plaint note
* fee of £20
* an additional fee of 15p per £ (minimum £5, maximum £30) where enforcement of arrears of rent is also sought.

A warrant is prepared and sealed by the court office. This instructs the bailiffs to take possession. The bailiff will fix a date for doing so and notify both plaintiff and defendant of the date. Unless an application is made to the court to suspend the warrant for possession, the bailiff will, on the day fixed, evict the tenant or occupier of the house.

The bailiff will require the plaintiff or his representative to sign the court warrant as a receipt for possession. The plaintiff is usually asked to have a locksmith available to change the locks to the house and also to secure the house against possible re-entry.

suspension of warrant for possession
The court has power to suspend a warrant on such terms as it thinks fit for possession of mortgaged property; for property held on a protected tenancy, a warrant can be suspended only where the court had a discretion whether or not to grant possession. (For example, in arrears cases, where an order for possession in 28 days was made originally, the court can suspend the warrant for possession if the defendant pays the arrears of rent or mortgage payments, by specified monthly instalments.)

Strictly, there is no power to suspend an order for possession in other cases, although applications are frequently made and the court will sometimes order that the warrant be not enforced, but for only a limited period of time.

going to court in Scotland

Most consumer cases are heard by the sheriff court. There is a sheriff court in each area, generally in the nearest city or major town (address and telephone number in the telephone directory).

There are two forms of action, depending on the value of your claim. For claims of £1,000 or less, the procedure used is called a 'summary cause'. For claims over that amount, the procedure used is an 'ordinary action'. The procedure for an ordinary action is more complicated than summary cause procedure and, although you are theoretically allowed to present your own case, the technicalities and time involved make it wiser to use a solicitor. Certainly you would need legal advice.

summary cause

The summary cause procedure was introduced to make it easier for people to represent themselves in court to settle small debts. Although it is simpler and less technical than an 'ordinary' action, the rules are still fairly complicated and you would be well advised to get some legal advice before representing yourself. You may be eligible for free or subsidised advice from a solicitor under the 'pink form' scheme for legal assistance.

A free leaflet available at sheriff courts, *Guide to the new summary cause in the sheriff court*, explains briefly how to begin an action, what to do if you get a summons, where to get advice.

filling in the forms

There are different forms for different kinds of claim. For instance, in a summary cause action for the payment of money (for example, claiming refund of the £75 paid for a faulty vacuum cleaner which the trader will not take back, or claiming return of a deposit of £100 paid for plumbing work which was never carried out), you will need to get summary cause form SC3 'action for payment' from the sheriff clerk at the court. If your claim is not for a money payment, the sheriff clerk will tell you what form to fill in, and may help you to do so.

On the form, you must put in your full name and address as 'pursuer' of the action. Then put in the name and address of the person you are suing – the 'defender' of the action.

If you are suing a business, you should write down the name of the firm, or the names of the partners if you know these, as well as the registered address. (All businesses should have a notice at their premises containing this information.) If the defender is a limited company, and you are not sure about its name or business address, the Registrar of Companies (102 George Street, Edinburgh EH2 3DJ) should be able to let you know what it is.

Make sure you sue the right person. There is no point in naming the shop assistant as defender when it is the company which is responsible.

how much to claim
The next part of the form to fill in is the amount you are claiming. In many cases, it is easy to decide what this sum should be. For example, if you pay £100 for a set of encyclopaedias and you neither receive them nor get your money back, the sum to claim will be £100. But suppose someone repairs your roof for £150 and, even after the repairs, the roof leaks and you have had to get another slater in to put it right, your claim should be for the cost of employing the other tradesman. So, if the later job costs £100, your claim should be for £100, not £100 plus the original £150.

You may find it difficult to work out exactly how much to claim. For example, if you hire a carpet cleaning machine which is defective and damages your carpet, you should claim the amount it will cost to repair the carpet. If the carpet is beyond repair, you should claim the value of the carpet before it was damaged, not the cost of buying a new one. This may be difficult to work out, but you have to try to do so. It is better not to underestimate because the most you will get is the amount you claim. If you make a slight overestimate, the court may reduce the amount when deciding on the claim.

You may be entitled to claim an additional amount for loss of earnings or travel expenses to see people about the problem or for any annoyance or inconvenience caused to you. If you made it clear at the beginning of the agreement that time was an essential part of the contract, you could be entitled to claim also for expenditure caused by the delay.

basis of claim

Next, the form has a space for you to set out in plain language the basis of your case against the defender. This is called the 'statement of claim'. Put down just the facts. For example, if the new washing machine does not work properly, you should state where and when you bought it, what the price was, in what way it is defective, and that you accordingly reject the machine and want your money back.

The completed form must be lodged with the sheriff clerk of the court for the area where the defendant lives or carries on business,. The sheriff clerk will tell you how much the appropriate court fee is.

serving the summons

When the form has been lodged, the sheriff clerk will insert the date on which the case is first to be heard and sign the summons, which he gives you. You are then entitled to cite the defender to appear in court.

To do this, you must serve on the defender a copy of the summons identical to the summons that the sheriff clerk has signed. On this will be the return date (the date before which the defender must reply, admitting the claim or not) and the calling date (when the case will first be heard in court).

You should send the summons to the defender by recorded delivery post or, alternatively, have it served by a sheriff officer (who will charge you a fee for doing so). Names of sheriff officers can be obtained from the sheriff clerk.

After you have served the copy summons, you must then complete on the original summons the part that states how you served the summons on the defender, along with the recorded delivery receipt if that is how you did it.

Before the return date, the date before which the defender must respond by either agreeing or disagreeing with your claim, you should return the completed summons to the sheriff clerk.

the defender

The defender's statement should be received by the court before the return date. He may admit the claim and perhaps offer to pay by instalments. If you agree, the claim can be settled then by notifying the court who may grant a decree on those terms without having to go through a court hearing. In this case, the defender will have to pay your expenses so far.

If you do not agree, you will have to turn up at the court hearing to argue for the original figure or amended instalments.

If the defender does not return the statement by the return date, you are entitled to ask that the fact be minuted in the court's summary cause book, along with a claim for a decree in your favour with expenses. In practice, most sheriff clerks allow the defender who is unrepresented by a solicitor to 'enter an appearance' right up to the date of the hearing.

the hearings

The calling day is when the case comes up for its first hearing, before the sheriff clerk. This is mainly an opportunity for the defender to state what his position is. A further date will be set to hear a 'proof' of the action before the sheriff, when you will have to bring along any witnesses.Written evidence should be lodged at court at least 7 days before the proof hearing, and a list sent to the defender.

proof hearing

At the proof hearing, you cannot just allege that certain things have been said or done. The truth of your statement must be established according to the rules of evidence and you will have to provide corroboration to establish your major points.

This means that you will require witnesses or written evidence, such as a written contract or a receipt, to back up your claims. Where you argue one point and the trader argues another, without witnesses or written evidence, it can be difficult for the court to establish the truth.

It is always worthwhile, where possible, to back up your claim with professional evidence. If, for example, you are claiming that the roof repairs were badly done and caused dampness in your house, you would need a surveyor's report or an estimate by another roof repairer. Photographs of the unsatisfactory work or product can sometimes be useful, too, but unless they are unequivocally dated, their value is limited.

If you cannot find an expert to evaluate the extent of your loss or the unsatisfactory nature of the work, your local consumer protection department may be able to put you in touch with one. The Scottish Consumer Council (314 St Vincent Street, Glasgow G3 8xw) has produced a guide to testing facilities which it might be worth trying to get hold of.

the basic procedure in court

Summary cause procedure is meant to be as simple as possible to allow the layperson to conduct his own action in court. To get a feel of the procedure, you can go and sit in on some other cases beforehand. You will find that the sheriff is likely to be sympathetic towards someone who is representing himself and to give what help he can within the procedural rules of the court.

As pursuer, you put your own case first, bringing in any witnesses or evidence you may have. The defender has the right to question you and your witnesses after this. Then the defender puts his own case, also bringing any witnesses or evidence that he considers relevant. You are entitled to question the defender and his witnesses. The sheriff may want to ask questions, too. The pursuer has to wind up by summarising his case.

The sheriff usually gives his judgment orally there and then, with a short written decision sent later. In cases where the sheriff requires more time to reach his decision, he sends it afterwards in writing.

defending a court action

You may have to go to court not because you are raising an action yourself but because you are being sued by a trader for money. This may be because you have defaulted on a credit contract, such as HP or personal loan, or because you have not paid a bill for goods or services that have been delivered to you.

In some cases, you may be taken to court for a debt that you are not prepared to pay – for example, where payment for unsatisfactory work is being demanded. In this case, you can either put in a counterclaim for damages or ask the court to decide that the work was unsatisfactory and that no further payment is due. The procedure is a mirror image of what happens when you are the pursuer.

When you are served a summons, either by recorded delivery post or by sheriff officer, you are given the return date before which you must reply saying whether or not you agree with the claim. The summons must be returned to the sheriff clerk, not to the pursuer.

If you are defending the action because you do not believe you should have to pay, you should take the precaution of keeping the money aside or lodging it with the court in case you lose the action. This may happen, however much in the right you feel you are.

If you do agree with the claim but cannot pay the full amount immediately, and do not want to come to court, complete form R (at the back of the summons) and make a written offer to repay by instalments. State your financial circumstances and the amount and dates on which instalments are to be paid. If the pursuer accepts this arrangement, you will have avoided an unnecessary appearance in court, but you will be liable for his legal expenses. The pursuer may, however, reject your offer of instalments and seek a decree for the full amount, or increased instalments. You may only find out when the pursuer takes steps to enforce the decree.

If you do not agree with the claim, you should complete form Q (at the back of the summons), giving reasons. You do not, however, have to list the witnesses you intend calling or the evidence you intend to bring before the court.

going to the hearing

It is important that you turn up in court for the first hearing. Failure to do so will almost inevitably result in a decree being granted against you. Even if you admit the debt, it is worth going to court so that you can argue for repayment by instalments because of your income and other commitments.

If you do not agree that you owe the money or if you dispute the amount of the debt, the case will be put back for a few weeks for a 'proof' hearing. This is the hearing at which you should bring in any witnesses or written evidence you may have.

losing the case

If you lose the action and decree is granted against you, you become liable for payment of the debt or for the agreed instalments. In most cases, you will have to pay the pursuer's legal expenses, as well as any of your own.

enforcement

Failure to pay as arranged could result in the pursuer getting what is called an 'extract' of the decree against you (this will be served on you by a sheriff officer). You have 14 days after this in which to pay up. If you do not, the pursuer can go ahead with procedure leading up to a warrant sale on your possessions. This means that a sheriff officer will value your property, perhaps at ridiculously low prices which may not cover the debt, and advertise the warrant sale. There is nothing you can do about this. Any item in your home which does not belong to you or which is being bought on hire-purchase cannot be sold, nor can certain basic belongings such as a bed, bedclothes and the tools of your trade. You are liable also for the sheriff officer's expenses. Repeated warrant sales can be held but no sale can take place more than a year after the initial decree was granted.

Alternatively, the pursuer can arrange for your wages to be arrested by instructing a firm of sheriff officers to ask your employer to deduct from your next wage for the debt. If there is a decree against you, your employer cannot refuse to deduct the money. You must be left with at least half your weekly earnings over £4. A fresh application must be made for each wage arrested.

Social security payments cannot be arrested in this way.

appeals

There is a right of appeal against the sheriff's decision, but only on the ground that proper procedure has not been complied with or if you disagree with a point of law in the case. You cannot appeal about decisions of fact. For example, if the sheriff decided that the fault on your washing machine is minor and the trader agrees to replace the faulty part, you cannot appeal against his decision on this. But if he decided that minor faults do not render the trader liable in any way at all, this would be an unusual and new way of interpreting the law and you would be within your rights to appeal against the judgment on a point of law.

Going to court in Scotland is based on text prepared by Ken Swinton for the Scottish Consumer Council.

in the High Court

To a large extent, the High Court deals with actions where there are difficult issues of fact and/or law involved and generally large sums of money in dispute.

Much of its procedure is based on the assumption that the parties will be legally represented. Although a litigant in person can, with some perseverance, deal with a simple claim or defence, very little is done to ease the path of the litigant in person. Some help can be obtained in the central office of the High Court at the Law Courts in London, where a citizens advice bureau is in operation.

The cost is a most important aspect of a High Court action. An unsuccessful party could be faced with a high bill of costs, and even if successful, is likely to end up with a considerable outlay that cannot be recovered.

A potential litigant should find out whether he is eligible for legal aid before he does anything. A citizens advice bureau will know about the current conditions and financial limits for eligibility. An application for legal aid involves an assessment of the legal merits of your case by the legal aid office.

The High Court is divided into the Queen's Bench Division, the Chancery Division and the Family Division. Most straightforward actions – for example, for payment of money due for goods supplied, for damages arising from a road accident, for damages for the supply of goods that were not of merchantable quality – take place in the Queen's Bench Division.

It would be unwise to bring a case in the High Court yourself where the amount of the damages claimed is not known ('unliquidated') – for example, a personal injuries case. But a stouthearted litigant in person could attempt to take a relatively straightforward case for a fixed sum of money ('liquidated damages').

In many cases, judgment is given without a full court hearing at a chambers hearing before a 'master' or a district registrar (usually known as an 'order 14' judgment).

starting proceedings in the Queen's Bench Division

Proceedings are started by preparing, issuing and serving a writ of summons. In simple actions, this one document performs the functions both of a summons and of a particulars of claim in the county court. There is no reason why the writ should not be typed out but a simpler course is to buy a writ form from a firm of law stationers. At the same time, it is sensible to obtain forms of acknowledgment of service, forms for entry of judgment and a form of order 14 summons and affidavit in support, together with spare copies for you to use for drafting.

The writ starts with the formal heading of the action:

IN THE HIGH COURT OF JUSTICE   No. 1985-B-0021
QUEEN'S BENCH DIVISION
(ANYTOWN DISTRICT REGISTRY)

BETWEEN

            John Brown   plaintiff
                and
     William Alfred Smith   defendant

The number is assigned by the court. It is made up of the year of issue, the first letter of the plaintiff's surname and a serial number.

An action can be started in the central office of the High Court in London at the Law Courts in the Strand, or in any district registry. If the action is commenced in London, the words '- - - - - - District Registry' should be struck out in the heading.

A district registry is a local office of the High Court where writs and summonses are issued and where most pre-trial hearings take place. Each district registry covers the districts of one or more county courts and the office is part of the county court office. Your local county court will be able to give you details of the district registry for any particular place. There are district registries in all substantial towns and cities.

You are entitled to issue a writ in any district registry or in the central office in London, whichever is more convenient to you. The rule for county courts that proceedings must be started in the county court in whose district either the defendant lives or in which the cause of action arose does not apply to the issue of proceedings in the High Court. The defendant, however, may apply to have the action transferred to

London or the district registry where he lives or where the cause of action arose.

The defendant's full names and address have to be stated in the writ (registered office if the defendant is a company). The writ warns the defendant that if he does not file an acknowledgment of service at the court office within 14 days of service of the writ, judgment may be entered against him.

The back of the writ contains the details of the claim, called in the High Court, the 'statement of claim'. This needs to be no more than a very general outline of the plaintiff's claim; the plaintiff will have to serve a full statement of claim separately after the defendant has filed the acknowledgment of service.

The drafting of the statement of claim follows similar lines to a particulars of claim in the county court, but drafting a claim in the High Court is much more important than in the county court where, traditionally, some latitude is allowed in pleadings, particularly where a party is not legally represented.

The completed writ is 'issued' by taking or sending to the central office or the district registry of your choice

* the top copy of the writ – dated and signed by the plaintiff
* a photostat copy (or other exact copy of the original) of the writ, with an extra copy for each defendant
* an acknowledgment of service for each defendant
* the fee of £55.

In practice, it is advisable to take rather than send these documents to the appropriate court office so that any errors can be corrected there and then.

The staff at the court office check the writ and acknowledgment of service to see that they appear to be correct and will then seal the documents and return to you one copy of the writ together with the further copies for each defendant and the acknowledgment(s) of service. The court office retains the original copy of the writ.

service

The next step is to serve the writ either personally, or through the post by sending (or by putting through the letterbox) one sealed copy of the writ and of the acknowledgment of service in an envelope addressed to the defendant. Writs can be served by post to the defendant's residence or place of business. The place of business applies only where the defendant is self-employed: service cannot be effected at the place where the defendant is employed.

The date of service is important. If there is no proof of date, service is deemed to be effected on the seventh day after posting – irrespective of when the defendant actually receives the writ.

Where the defendant is a limited company, the writ and acknowledgment of service must be sent to the registered office of the company. Service is deemed to be effected on the second day after posting if first class post is used, or the fourth day if second class post is used.

Where the writ and acknowledgment of service are handed personally to the defendant, there is no 'deemed' date of service: the actual date of personal service is what counts.

what the defendant does
The next step depends on whether or not the defendant completes the acknowledgment of service and returns it to the court (in which case, a copy is sent on to you) and whether he indicates an intention to defend if he does return the acknowledgment.

If the acknowledgment of service is not returned within 14 days of deemed or actual date of service, the plaintiff can ask for judgment to be entered against the defendant. This is done by the plaintiff filing at the court office an affidavit of service, stating when the writ was posted to the defendant (and by which class post in the case of a limited company) and two copies of the form of default judgment (obtainable also from law stationers). Provided that the acknowledgment of service has not in the meanwhile been received by the court, judgment will be entered and a sealed copy of the judgment returned to you. No notification is given to the defendant that judgment has been entered against him. You can proceed immediately to enforce judgment, or you can write to the defendant telling him and saying that unless he pays up within, say, a week you will take steps to enforce the judgment.

If the defendant has returned the acknowledgment of service stating that he does not wish to defend, the procedure to get judgment is the same, except that you will not have to bother about filing an affidavit of service.

defendant defending
If the defendant indicates that he wants to defend, he must serve on you a copy of his defence within 14 days of the expiration of the time for filing the acknowledgment of service. If he cannot get a defence prepared within the allotted number of days, the defendant can send a letter to the plaintiff asking for an extension of time for the defence,

generally an extension of between 14 and 28 days (depending on the complexity of the case).

If the plaintiff does not allow the requested extension, the defendant can apply to the court where the writ was issued, on a form of summons, for an extension of time. The summons is then sent to the plaintiff with a note of the date of the hearing. Courts normally allow one extension (if not already granted by the plaintiff) without difficulty, but need to be satisfied that there is justification for any further extension.

In drafting his defence, the defendant must make sure that he makes clear that he disputes those parts of the claim against him which he is not prepared to admit. The rules of pleading in the High Court provide that anything in the statement of claim which is not denied, is to be regarded as admitted. So, the defendant should state clearly which paragraphs of the statement of claim he admits and which he denies, and then state concisely the facts on which he will rely to defend the claims made against him. Because it is so important to deny all allegations that are not admitted, it is usual to finish off a defence by saying "Save as hereinbefore specifically admitted, the defendant denies each and every allegation contained in the statement of claim as though each were herein set out seriatim and specifically traversed" (this means as though each allegation were listed and expressly con-tradicted).

If the defendant wishes to make a claim against the plaintiff – a counterclaim – this should be included in the same document as the defence.

If the defendant fails to serve his defence within the appropriate time, the plaintiff may ask for judgment in default by completing and sending to the court the form of default judgment, on which the plaintiff must confirm that no defence has been served on him within the time prescribed (or any extension of that time granted by the court or the plaintiff). The court then seals and issues the order for judgment.

an 'order 14' summons

Where the defendant states that he intends to defend the claim against him, but the plaintiff feels that his own case is so strong that the defendant is merely playing for time, the plaintiff can, without waiting for a defence to be served, apply to the court for summary judgment under order 14 of the Rules of the Supreme Court.

The forms for an order 14 summons and affidavit in support can be obtained from law stationers. The summons has to be completed by filling in the headings as on the writ and dating and signing it. The affidavit in its simplest form just needs to have the heading and the amount of the claim inserted, and to be sworn before a solicitor (for a fee) or a member of the court staff. If the defendant has indicated his defence, it is sensible to give more detailed evidence in the affidavit, attaching ('exhibiting') any documents, such as letters and invoices, to show that the defendant really has no defence.

Two copies of the summons, and the original of the affidavit, should be taken to the court office. The summons will be sealed, and the date fixed for the hearing inserted. You should then serve the summons and a copy of your affidavit on the defendant.

The defendant may file an affidavit in answer showing that he has an 'arguable defence'; if there is time, you can prepare and swear an affidavit disputing in as much detail as possible what the defendant says in his affidavit.

hearing of 'order 14' summons

The hearing of the summons is before a master in the central office of the High Court or a district registrar in a district registry. Usually, the hearing takes only a few minutes. The master will probably read any affidavits that have been filed and then allow each side – plaintiff first, then the defendant if he has turned up, and then the plaintiff having the last word – to put arguments to him as to whether or not there is an arguable or triable issue.

The master's job is not to try the case but to see whether on the evidence before him there is a genuine dispute that ought to be tried. For example, if the defendant says that goods for which the plaintiff is claiming payment were not of merchantable quality, the master cannot go into that issue but he might be persuaded that there was no triable issue if he were given evidence to show that the defendant had been using the goods without complaint for a considerable time.

The master may decide

• that there is no triable issue and that the plaintiff is entitled to judgment

• that there is a triable issue and that the action should proceed

• that the plaintiff should have judgment for part of his claim but that there is a triable issue as to the balance and there should be a trial as to that balance

• that although he feels bound to say that there is a triable issue, he feels that the defendant's case is so weak and unlikely to succeed that he imposes a condition on giving leave to defend – usually the payment into court to 'abide the event' of all or part of the money claimed. In this case, the money paid into court remains there until the action is tried: if the plaintiff is successful, the money is then paid out to him; if not, it is returned to the defendant.

If the master does not give judgment for all that the plaintiff is claiming, the master should be asked to give directions for trial. These are similar to the directions for trial in the county court. There are, however, two other directions that the master can give which can lead to a more economical and speedy trial.

He can transfer the action to the county court, even if the amount involved is more than £5,000. (This is likely to make it easier for a litigant in person to conduct his own case.) He will not do this unless he is satisfied that there are no exceptionally complicated issues of fact or law which would make it desirable for the case to be heard by a High Court judge.

Or the master can order – if both parties agree – that the action be tried by himself instead of by a High Court judge. Such a trial will be in open court and all the normal rules of evidence and procedure will apply but it often means a much earlier trial than a hearing before a High Court judge. (The gap between setting down and hearing of normal High Court trials is usually in excess of six months.)

It is the duty of the plaintiff to have the order 14 drawn up. This means that he has to prepare a document which has the heading as on the writ and then goes on to set out the terms of the order. The Queen's Bench masters have prepared practice forms for all the usual orders on an order 14 summons (and other types of summonses) and these can be found in volume 2 of what is known as the 'white book' – more correctly, the *Supreme Court Practice*. Most courts will allow you to inspect a copy and take a note of the appropriate form; the 'white book' may also be available in larger reference libraries.

Take three copies of the order to the court office, where the staff will
check and seal them. One copy is retained by the court and two copies
returned: one for you and one to serve on the defendant.

There are some differences in procedure on summonses between the
central office and district registries. In the former, affidavits – previously sealed by the court office – are normally handed to the master at
the hearing. In district registries, the normal practice is to file the
affidavits before the hearing. In the central office, you should also hand
to the master at the beginning of the hearing the original summons. He
will then endorse the order on that summons, which you have to
produce to the court staff when having the order sealed. In district
registries, it is not usually necessary to hand in the original summons –
the district registrar notes his order on the court file.

enforcement

Judgment can be enforced in the High Court by not dissimilar methods
to those in the county court. (One method of enforcement is to have the
action transferred to the county court for enforcement, by an attachment
of earnings order.)

The most usual form of enforcement is the issue of a writ of 'fiere
facias' (fi. fa.), which is very similar to a warrant of execution in the
county court.

A form of praecipe (or request) for issuing of a writ of fi. fa. and the
form of writ itself (obtainable from law stationers) should be completed
and taken to the central office or to the district registry where judgment
was entered, together with a sealed copy of the judgment and a fee of £6.

The court office, after checking the documents, will seal the writ of fi.
fa. and return it to you.

You should then send the writ of fi. fa. with a fee of £2.30 to the under
sheriff for the county in which the writ is to be executed – that is, the
county in which the defendant's assets which are to be seized are
situated. (The addresses of under sheriffs are in the Law List, which
should be at your local reference library.) It is important to give the
under sheriff as much information as possible about the debtor and any
assets he may have, in the letter accompanying the writ of fi. fa.

The under sheriff then issues a warrant for one of his bailiffs or
officers to enforce the judgment by seizure of sufficient goods of the
defendant to cover the judgment debt and costs, any accrued interest

(from date of judgment to date of payment), the sheriff's charges, the fee on a writ of fi. fa. and the expenses of removal and sale.

The under sheriff will acknowledge the writ and let you know which officer is dealing with the warrant; you should telephone the officer for reports of progress.

A visit by a sheriff's officer with a writ of fi. fa. may be sufficient to persuade the defendant to pay up, or at least make proposals to pay by substantial instalments. If not, the sheriff's officer will arrange for the removal and sale of sufficient of the defendant's assets. The sheriff's officer is entitled to deduct his own costs from the net proceeds of the sale. The under sheriff must hold on to the balance for 14 days in case any steps should be taken to make the defendant bankrupt, in which case he would have to pay the money he has recovered to the receiver. Otherwise, the under sheriff will pay to the creditor sufficient money to cover the judgment debt, costs and interest and fi. fa. fee. Any surplus is paid to the defendant – unless the under sheriff knows of other writs of fi. fa. or county court warrants of execution, in which case he will pay those off in date order.

If the execution is abortive, the creditor will receive a bill from the sheriff's officer for work done (£15 to £35), and should insist on a full report about the debtor.

getting legal advice

If, after the hearing of the order 14 summons, the whole action is to proceed to be tried by a High Court judge, you should take legal advice, whether you are the plaintiff or defendant.

Conducting an action in the High Court can be a daunting experience for trained lawyers, let alone the average layman. The judge will be unsympathetic to any wasting of the court's time and an experienced counsel on the other side will almost certainly leave the litigant in person tied up in knots and not knowing what to do next. Moreover, the risk in costs if a serious procedural mistake is made by a litigant in person are considerable. In most cases, legal representation is essential.

in a magistrates' court

All criminal cases in England and Wales begin by proceedings in the magistrates' courts; over 97% of defendants are dealt with and sentenced in these courts. The most serious cases are sent to the crown court which offers jury trial, and has much greater sentencing powers.

Magistrates try not only adults (anyone aged 17 years and over), but also have power to try juveniles (those from 10 to 16 years). Juvenile offenders appear in a special juvenile court, unless the case also involves an adult.

civil cases

Magistrates also have a civil jurisdiction. Care proceedings in respect of all young people under the age of 17 years take place in the juvenile court.

Magistrates may make guardianship orders for children whether or not the parents are married, and have power to make custodianship orders for someone who cares for a child (for example, foster parents). They may also make domestic protection orders against violent marriage partners.

Magistrates also adjudicate in domestic courts dealing with cases where matrimonial disputes have arisen. For example, if a husband has left his wife, magistrates may make orders relating to the maintenance of wife and children and to access and the custody of children. If the paternity of an illegitimate child has been established, they can make what is called an affiliation order to provide for the maintenance of the child.

The magistrates' civil jurisdiction also covers the licensing of public houses and off-sales, the granting of gaming licences and bookmakers' and betting shop licences, the recovery of unpaid rates and certain debts.

Also, if the magistrates have awarded costs to a litigant which have not been paid by the other party, those costs may be enforced in the magistrates' court.

who are magistrates?

The Lord Chancellor appoints magistrates. Local advisory committees (of which there are about 100 throughout the country) put forward the names of people regarded as suitable to become magistrates. Any person or organisation may recommend a candidate for appointment as a magistrate; recommendation forms are available from the secretary of a local advisory committee, or from the clerk of the local magistrates' court.

The paramount consideration in selecting magistrates is that they should be personally suitable in character, integrity and understanding for the work which they have to perform, and that they should be generally recognised as such by those among whom they live and work.

Lay magistrates are unpaid. Employment protection legislation safeguards the rights of citizens to have time off from work to serve as magistrates.

Any british subject under the age of 60 is eligible to be appointed as a magistrate, with specified exceptions, such as an undischarged bankrupt or a person convicted of certain offences.

It is unusual for anyone over the age of 55 to be appointed a magistrate or for one to stay on after the age of 70. Where possible, all benches contain a proportion of men and women in their thirties.

Political views of candidates are one of the considerations when making appointments; the Lord Chancellor and his advisory committees recognise the need to make each bench broadly representative of the community it serves.

Magistrates are frequently requested by members of the public to sign various documents. Fees may not be taken by magistrates for performing these duties.

Most magistrates' courts are composed of three lay magistrates; when sitting as a juvenile or domestic court, there must be at least one man and one woman on the bench. In some courts in the larger urban areas, notably in London, there is a full-time, legally qualified stipendiary (paid) magistrate, who sits alone.

Normally, magistrates are not legally qualified and are advised by the clerk to the justices on legal and procedural matters, both in and out of court. The justices' clerk must be a barrister or solicitor of at least 5 years' standing, and his court clerks must either be qualified as barristers or solicitors or hold a diploma in magisterial law.

The court staff will answer questions from members of the public on matters of law and procedure in magistrates' courts. But if the issue is at all complex, they will probably suggest seeking the advice of a solicitor and will supply a list of solicitors and give information on the 'green form' legal advice and assistance scheme.

No two magistrates' courts are ever exactly alike.

criminal trials

The great majority of criminal offences are investigated by the police and prosecuted by them or by lawyers acting on their behalf. The police do not, however, have an exclusive right either to investigate or to prosecute offences. Government departments, local authorities and other public bodies also conduct investigations and bring prosecutions for certain types of offence – for example, customs and excise offences, social security offences and breaches of consumer protection legislation.

Some offences (for example, relating to weights and measures) can be prosecuted only by particular public authorities. Where no such restriction exists, however, a private citizen may carry out his own enquiries into an offence, can initiate proceedings and in many cases is entitled to conduct the prosecution himself. There are exceptional circumstances where a private person may arrest someone who has committed – or whom he has reasonable grounds for suspecting of having committed – a serious offence, such as burglary, theft, wounding, damage. He should tell the accused why he has been arrested and then make immediate arrangements to hand the accused over to the police.

A private individual may initiate criminal proceedings by going to the local magistrates' court to 'lay an information', setting out details of the offences alleged and of the defendant who is alleged to have committed them. That information will be placed before a magistrate or the justices' clerk to consider whether to issue a summons against the alleged offender.

before the trial

When an application for a summons is granted, the summons is served on the accused, requiring him to attend court at a stated time to answer the information that has been laid before the court. For certain minor offences, he may be given the opportunity, if he admits the offence, to plead guilty by post without attending the court in person.

Where a person has been arrested, he will usually be charged instead of summonsed: he may then be kept in custody or released on bail until the court appearance.

When the defendant appears before a magistrates' court, the court may establish whether it should try the case itself or send it to the crown court for trial. Most minor offences, called summary offences (for example, many of the traffic offences), are triable only by a magistrates' court. The most serious offences (for example, murder, rape, robbery) are called indictable offences, and are triable only at the crown court.

There is, however, a large intermediate group of offences, including theft and burglary, which are triable either summarily by magistrates or on indictment by the crown court. The magistrates decide which of the two methods of trial seems most appropriate on the facts. Both the prosecution and the accused can make representations about this. If the magistrates decide on summary trial, the accused may refuse and choose trial by jury in the crown court, but if the magistrates announce crown court trial, the accused cannot insist on summary trial. In practice, the majority of these 'either way' cases are dealt with by magistrates.

In general, the maximum sentence which magistrates may impose for a single offence is six months' imprisonment and a fine of £2,000; for many summary offences, the maxima are lower. In the case of an offence which is triable either way, in which it has been agreed that the accused should be tried by the magistrates, if the magistrates find the accused guilty, they then (not before) hear about his previous convictions for this type of offence. If they then consider that their own sentencing powers are inadequate, they may commit the accused to the crown court for sentence: the crown court has power to impose higher penalties.

committal proceedings

All criminal cases begin in the magistrates' court. Even if the defendant is to be tried on indictment before the crown court, magistrates will first conduct an examination called 'committal proceedings'.

Committal proceedings are conducted by one or more magistrates sitting as examining justices. Their purpose is not to try the case but to decide whether there is sufficient evidence to put before a jury in a crown court for trial.

Full committal proceedings are used in only a small minority of cases to discover whether there is sufficient evidence to establish that the accused person has a case to answer. Committal without consideration of evidence may only be used if the accused is legally represented before the magistrates and consents to the procedure.

summary trial

The trial takes place before a single stipendiary magistrate or before a bench of, usually three, lay magistrates. There is no jury in a magistrates' court.

It is the task of the magistrates to listen to the evidence and assess the facts on both sides. Throughout, they receive the advice of the clerk to the justices as to the law and the extent of their powers.

The prosecution may be conducted by a barrister or a solicitor, or a police officer may prosecute. A private prosecution may be conducted by the person who has initiated the proceedings.

defendant

The summons tells you the date and time you are to be at the court. If you were charged and released on bail, the bail document will tell you this.

If the defendant fails to answer a summons, the court can, subject to certain safeguards, try the case in his absence or, if it considers his presence is necessary, it may issue a warrant for his arrest.

A defendant of limited means who wants to be represented by a barrister or solicitor may apply for legal aid.

legal aid

Applications for legal aid must be made to the clerk to the justices or to the court itself.

The Law Society has issued a booklet *Legal Aid Guide* and a leaflet *Legal Aid for Criminal Offences* (both available from citizens advice bureaux), which give details of the legal aid scheme, and who may be eligible. They tell you to apply as soon as possible to the court that is dealing with the case. The court will supply you with the necessary application form for legal aid, in which you will be asked to give details of your income and savings.

The court will decide whether

★ it is in the interests of justice that you should have legal representation
★ you require help in paying for it.

If the court decides that you can afford it, you may be asked to pay towards your costs at the end of the case. You may even be required to make a payment before being granted criminal legal aid.

Some courts have a duty solicitor who can provide legal advice and representation for the first appearance, and whose services are free.

at the trial

When you arrive at the court, look for a list of cases posted on a notice-board, so that you can see in which court you are to appear. Tell the court usher or the police officer that you are present and then wait, either in the courtroom or outside, until your name is called. There is no guarantee that cases will be called in the order in which they appear on the list.

When your name is called, go into the courtroom; you will be told where to stand. The person sitting in front, and usually a little below the magistrates, is the justices' clerk.

A defendant is asked to take the oath or to affirm. The charge or summons is read out. After any necessary decision about summary trial if it is an 'either way' offence, you will be asked whether you plead guilty or not guilty.

If you plead 'guilty', you can put forward a plea in mitigation before the magistrates decide the penalty. A mitigation plea should set out reasons why the fine or other punishment should be less severe than it would otherwise be.

If you plead 'not guilty', the evidence is called. You will be given an opportunity to ask questions of each witness and to address the court. A witness can be called to give evidence for either the prosecution or for the defence, and can be cross-examined by the other side as well. The magistrates can also put questions.

If you wish to call any witnesses to support your case, make sure that you have warned them to come to the court on the date when the 'not guilty' plea will be heard. You should tell them that they will have to leave the court immediately after you have pleaded 'not guilty' at the beginning of the trial. (All witnesses are normally ordered to leave the court at this point.) Although you can call as witness someone who has remained in court, that person's evidence may not carry much weight if he has heard the evidence given by other witnesses and could therefore be thought to have altered his own story.

First, the prosecutor calls his witnesses. When a prosecution witness has given his evidence, you are given the opportunity of asking any questions relevant to his evidence – that is, cross-examining the witness.

The object of asking questions is to try to obtain from the witness an admission that something he has said is not true, or that something he saw could have a different construction put on it. If you disagree with a point, make this clear by asking a question about it (unless the answer the witness may give is liable to undermine your case).

During the cross-examination, you are not allowed to make statements – you must ask questions. So, if a witness in a motoring case has given evidence that he saw you driving a green Metro and you were, in fact, driving a red Fiesta, do not say "My car is not a green Metro, it is a red Fiesta". You must ask a question to make clear that you disagree. For instance, ask "Are you quite sure that the car I was driving was a green Metro?" You must accept the witness's answer but you can try to demonstrate that it is wrong, by asking another question.

At the end of the prosecution case, an accused may submit (that is, say) that "there is no case to answer" if it seems that the prosecution have not produced sufficient evidence to prove their case. Or he may elect to give evidence.

If you wish to present evidence, you will generally be expected to give your own evidence first, and then to call your witnesses and question them. It is important not to ask a question which, by the way it is worded, suggests to your witness the reply that you wish to receive (a 'leading' question). For example, you may not say to the witness

"Will you tell the court that at 10pm last friday I was in the Blue Anchor with you?". But you can ask "Where were you at 10pm last friday?" and then "Were you alone?" and then "Who were you with?". If all goes well, you will get the answers that make it clear that at 10pm last friday the witness was in the Blue Anchor with you.

At the end of the prosecution's case, an accused may exercise his right of silence. This means that he cannot be compelled by the court to give evidence or to make any statement. This enables the accused to plead not guilty to the charge alleged against him but not to give evidence or to call any witnesses. If the prosecution case was a strong one, however, this would lead automatically to a conviction.

If you are found guilty, or pleaded guilty at the outset, sentence is passed by the magistrates after hearing from you any plea in mitigation. They also hear reports about an accused's character and are told of any previous convictions.

costs

If the accused is found guilty by the court, he can be ordered to pay the 'just and reasonable' costs incurred by the prosecutor in bringing the case before the court. Similarly, if the accused is acquitted, he may ask the court to order the prosecution to pay his costs, including his own travelling and subsistence expenses and loss of earnings. The costs may include not only a lawyer's fee for presenting the case but also costs of preparing the paperwork in the case, enquiries, witnesses attending court to give evidence, reports from experts.

All awards of costs are discretionary and the magistrates are not bound to order full reimbursement. The court will assess the amount of any costs between parties there and then.

The accused who is acquitted in an indictable case that is tried before magistrates, may ask the court to award him costs from central funds. An order will similarly be made for prosecution costs to be paid from central funds, unless the prosecution was brought unreasonably, whether it was successful or not. An accused, whether he was acquitted or not, may ask for his witnesses' costs to be paid in this way. The magistrates will make an order, leaving the actual amount to be assessed by the justices' clerk. There are restrictions on what can be ordered (for example, loss of earnings cannot be compensated) and there are ceilings on amounts.

private prosecutions

At a trial where an individual private citizen is the prosecutor, he can start by addressing the magistrates, setting out the circumstances of the offence alleged against the defendant.

He then calls and examines his witnesses, who may be cross-examined by the defendant or his legal representative. At the end of that cross-examination, the 'prosecutor' will be given an opportunity to re-examine his witnesses with a view to clarifying any ambiguity that may have arisen as a result of the cross-examination.

The defendant has the right then to give evidence and to call any witnesses, and the 'prosecutor' will be able to ask any relevant questions of the witnesses so called. The defendant or his legal representative at the conclusion of the case for the defence may address the court on the facts of the case; the 'prosecutor' has the right to address the court on matters of law only.

No cost arises in launching a private prosecution because no court fees are payable. If the defendant is acquitted, however, it will be open to him to apply to the court for his costs to be paid, either by the 'prosecutor' or, in an indictable case, from central funds.

right of appeal

A person convicted by a magistrates' court has a right of appeal to the crown court against conviction (unless he pleaded guilty) and/or against his sentence.

When the crown court hears such an appeal, the bench consists of a judge and, normally, two magistrates, and the proceedings take the form of a complete re-hearing of the case.

In addition to the defendant being able to appeal to the crown court, either party, including the prosecutor, may appeal direct to the High Court if it is thought that the magistrates have made a mistake as to the law.

domestic and juvenile cases

When magistrates sit to deal with family cases, either a civil case dealing with husband and wife or children, or a criminal case involving offenders aged from 10 to 16 inclusive, they are kept separate from other proceedings and the general public is excluded. The only people admitted are

- members and officers of the court
- the parties, their solicitors and counsel and witnesses and other persons directly concerned in that case
- the press (although it is forbidden to publish the evidence in a domestic case and any identification of a juvenile in a juvenile court)
- anyone else with special authorisation (a domestic court may not exclude anyone with adequate grounds for attending).

In adoption hearings, only the members and officers of the court, the parties and their lawyers are allowed to be present.

Legal aid may be granted to take or defend civil proceedings: applications (except in the case of care proceedings in the juvenile court which are made to the court itself) have to be made to the Law Society through a solicitor.

procedure

Civil proceedings in magistrates' courts are started by the making of a complaint, followed by the issue of a summons. The complaint need not be in writing, and may be made by the complainant in person, or by his or her legal representative or some other person authorised on his or her behalf.

After a complaint is made, a magistrate or the justices' clerk decides whether or not the court has power to make the order for which application is made and, if so, will issue a summons for the defendant to come before the court.

A time and place will be appointed for the hearing. If the defendant appears, the court will put the substance of each complaint to him. He is not obliged to admit or deny what is alleged but it would unnecessarily prolong the hearing and increase costs where there was no reason not to respond.

The complainant may then explain his or her case. In some circumstances, the court can make an order without hearing any evidence, but where this does not apply, the complainant will then call evidence. Evidence must be given on oath or affirmation. Neither party can be compelled to give evidence on his own behalf but in civil proceedings (unlike criminal proceedings), the defendant may be called as a witness by the complainant.

The complainant himself will usually give evidence, followed by his witnesses. All may be cross-examined in turn by the defendant, followed by re-examination to clear up any matters raised in cross-examination.

The defendant has to be careful about saying that there is 'no case to answer' at the end of the complainant's case because he may then be prevented from calling any evidence himself.

Subject to this, the defendant will then give his evidence and call his witnesses, with cross-examination and re-examination as before. He then ends with a speech summing up his case before the magistrates come to their decision.

Costs in civil proceedings are normally payable by the unsuccessful party to the successful party. But where the court has made an order for maintenance payments, it may order the successful party to pay the costs.

industrial tribunal

The industrial tribunals were set up to provide a cheap, speedy and informal forum for resolving employment disputes, with the idea that claimants would be able to represent themselves. Although the procedure adopted by tribunals is more informal than that adopted by the courts of law, the aim of providing a cheap, speedy and informal system has been only partially realised.

This is partly because of the complexity of the law which the tribunals have to administer and partly because legal representation has become quite common in tribunals, particularly on the part of employers. This has not helped to render the system more informal and tends to make things more difficult for the unrepresented claimant in an industrial tribunal.

have you a case?

The greatest difficulty is often the complexity of the law itself. Some areas are a minefield for the expert, let alone the layman. The principal statutes that apply are

Employment Protection Act 1975 (as amended)

Employment Protection (Consolidation) Act 1978 (as amended)

Employment Act 1980 (as amended)

Employment Act 1982

Equal Pay Act 1970 (as amended)

Sex Discrimination Act 1975

Race Relations Act 1976

Health and Safety at Work etc. Act 1974.

There are free leaflets on employment legislation issued by the Department of Employment which will give you some basic guidance as to the law.

1. *Written statement of main terms and conditions of employment*
2. *Procedure for handling redundancies*
3. *Employee's rights on insolvency of employer*
4. *Employment rights for the expectant mother*
5. *Suspension on medical grounds under health and safety regulations*
6. *Facing redundancy? – time off for job hunting or to arrange training*
7. *Union membership rights and the closed shop*
8. *Itemized pay statement*
9. *Guarantee payments*
10. *Employment rights on the transfer of an undertaking*
11. *Rules governing continuous employment and a week's pay*
12. *Time off for public duties*
13. *Unfairly dismissed?*
14. *Rights to notice and reasons for dismissal*
15. *Union secret ballots*
16. *Redundancy payments*

These can be obtained free from employment offices, jobcentres, unemployment benefit offices, and also other free publications (such as the guides to the Sex Discrimination Act and the Equal Pay Act) issued by the Department of Employment.

A free booklet issued by the Central Office of the Industrial Tribunals, *Industrial Tribunals Procedure* (ITL 1), lists the matters that an industrial tribunal may be asked to decide. These include

equal pay: right to receive the same pay and other terms of employment as an employee of the opposite sex working for the same or an associated employer if engaged on like work; work rated as equivalent under job evaluation or work of equal value (see *Equal pay – a guide to the Equal Pay Act*)

guarantee payments: right to receive guarantee pay from employer during lay-offs (see *employment legislation leaflet No. 9*)

insolvency of employer: right to be paid by the Secretary of State certain debts owed by an insolvent employer (see *employment legislation leaflet No. 3*)

itemised pay statement: right to receive an itemised pay statement
(see *employment legislation leaflet No. 8*)

maternity rights: right not to be unfairly dismissed for reasons connected with pregnancy, right to paid time off work for ante-natal care,
right to return to work following absence because of maternity;
right to receive maternity pay
(see *employment legislation leaflet No. 4*)

medical suspension: right not to be unfairly dismissed on suspension
on medical grounds relating to health and safety regulations;
right to receive pay on suspension on medical grounds
(see *employment legislation leaflet No. 5*)

race relations: right not to be discriminated against or victimised on
grounds of colour, race, nationality or ethnic or national origins
(see *Racial discrimination – a guide to the Race Relations Act* available from
the Commission for Racial Equality)

redundancy: right to receive payment under a protective award made
by an industrial tribunal;
right to receive redundancy payment or rebate, and questions relating
to the amount of such payments
(see *employment legislation leaflets No. 2 and 16*)

sex discrimination: right not to be discriminated against or victimised on the grounds of sex or marriage
(see *Sex discrimination – a guide to the Sex Discrimination Act*)

time off: right to paid time off for safety representatives;
right to time off for public duties;
right to paid time off in the event of redundancy to look for other work
or to make arrangements for training
(see *employment legislation leaflets No. 6 and 12*)

trade union membership/non-membership: right to paid time off for
trade union duties; right to time off for trade union activities;
right not to suffer action short of dismissal for trade union membership
or activities; right not to suffer action short of dismissal to compel
union membership or payments in lieu of membership;
right not to be unfairly dismissed for trade union membership or
activities; right not to be unfairly dismissed for non-membership of a
union whether inside or outside a closed shop;
right not to be chosen for redundancy because of trade union membership or activities or non-membership of a trade union whether inside
or outside a closed shop;

application for interim relief from an employee who has been unfairly dismissed for non-membership of a union or for trade union membership or activities;
right not to be unreasonably excluded or expelled from a union in a closed shop
(see *employment legislation leaflet No. 7* and a brief guide *Industrial action and the law*)

transfer of undertakings: right not to be dismissed on the transfer of an undertaking to a new employer except for certain reasons
(see *employment legislation leaflet No. 10*)

unfair dismissal: right not to be unfairly dismissed;
right to receive a written statement of reasons for dismissal
(see *employment legislation leaflets No. 13 and 14*)

written statement: right to receive a written statement of terms of employment or any alteration to them with sufficient details
(see *employment legislation leaflet No. 1*)

sources of advice

There are a number of sources of advice, including

trade unions
Trade unions have a considerable degree of experience in industrial tribunal matters. So, if you are a union member, you should approach your union for advice. The union may also be able to provide someone to represent you later at a tribunal hearing.

legal advice
You may be able to obtain free or partially free legal advice from a solicitor on the validity of your claim under the 'green form' scheme ('pink' in Scotland) if your financial resources are below the set limits. Or you may be able to obtain a solicitor's advice on your claim in a fixed-fee interview (£5 for half an hour). Legal aid is not available for a solicitor to represent you before an industrial tribunal.
   Voluntary organisations who can provide legal advice and possibly someone to represent you at a tribunal include citizens advice bureaux and local law centres. The Law Centres Federation (Duchess House, 18-19 Warren Street, London W1P 5DB) can provide a list of law centres and information about their work.

Advisory, Conciliation and Arbitration Service (ACAS)

ACAS provides information and advice on a wide range of employment, personnel and industrial relations matters. Confidential free advice can be obtained from the regional telephone enquiry points (the numbers are in the telephone directory) which cover all of England, Scotland and Wales. In Northern Ireland, a similar function is carried out by the Labour Relations Agency.

A booklet *Conciliation by ACAS in complaints by individuals to industrial tribunals* is available free from ACAS regional offices or the head office 11-12 St James's Square, London SW1Y 4LA (telephone: 01-214 6000), and also all the leaflets on employment legislation issued by the Department of Employment.

Equal Opportunities Commission

The Equal Opportunities Commission can help with problems and may also pay for legal representation if a case raises a point of principle or is complex. The address is Overseas House, Quay Street, Manchester M3 3HN (telephone: 061-833 9244). There are regional offices at 249 West George Street, Glasgow G2 4QE and Caerwys House, Windsor Lane, Cardiff CF1 1LB.

The EOC has a free booklet: *Sex discrimination and equal pay: how to prepare your own case for an industrial tribunal.*

The Commission for Racial Equality

If a case seems to involve racial discrimination, the CRE can be asked to provide advice and assistance, which in appropriate cases includes full legal representation. A guide to the Race Relations Act and a loose-leaf kit on presenting race cases in tribunals are available free from the CRE, Elliot House, 10-12 Allington Street, London SW1E 5EH (telephone: 01-828 7022).

composition of industrial tribunals

The industrial tribunal system is administered by the Central Office of the Industrial Tribunals (COIT): for England and Wales at 93 Ebury Bridge Road, London SW1W 8RE and for Scotland at St Andrew House, 141 West Nile Street, Glasgow G1 2RU. The Central Office is the body to which the initial application is made; a regional office of the industrial tribunals (ROIT) then deals with the application, including the hearing.

At present, there are regional offices in Birmingham, Bristol, Bury St Edmunds, Cardiff, Leeds, Liverpool, London (central, south and north), Manchester, Newcastle upon Tyne, Nottingham, Sheffield, Southampton, some with a sub-office where hearings may be held; in Scotland, Glasgow, Edinburgh, Aberdeen and Dundee.

An industrial tribunal itself is generally composed of a chairman and two lay members, although it can be validly constituted by a chairman and one lay member if both sides give their consent. The chairman is a barrister (advocate in Scotland) or solicitor of at least 7 years' standing.

The lay members are appointed by the Secretary of State for Employment. One member will be drawn from a panel of employer representatives and the other will be drawn from a panel of employee representatives. The function of the lay representatives is primarily to provide industrial experience and an awareness of the background against which employment law operates. Their function is not to provide active support for their own particular side of industry; they are neutral.

In a case involving sex discrimination, there will be both a man and a woman lay member; in a case involving racial discrimination, usually one lay member with special experience of race relations will be selected.

If proceedings were conducted by a tribunal consisting solely of lay members, there would be a danger of inconsistency and appeals on the grounds of error of law. The law is complex and parties are frequently unrepresented, and it is thought that it would be difficult for industrial tribunals to operate fairly or efficiently unless the proceedings were controlled by a legally qualified chairman.

Although the chairman tends to take the predominant role at the hearing, the lay members play a large part, usually taking notes and asking questions. Each member has an equal vote in the tribunal decision, so it is possible (although rare) for the chairman to be outvoted by the laymen. Where there is a tribunal of two, the chairman has the casting vote. Each industrial tribunal has a clerk (who is not legally qualified and has no judicial role) to carry out administrative functions.

starting a case

The basis for the procedure at industrial tribunals is contained in the Industrial Tribunal (Rules of Procedure) Regulations 1985 (Statutory Instrument 1985 No. 16; No. 17 for Scotland), which came into force on 1 March 1985. In Northern Ireland, the SI is 1981 No. 188. These regulations may be obtainable at a reference library.

The rules of procedure set out the method for making an application to an industrial tribunal. First of all, the applicant must write to the Secretary of Tribunals at the Central Office of the Industrial Tribunals stating his name and address, the name and address of the person against whom he is claiming and the grounds of what is claimed, with particulars. It is possible to initiate a claim by simply writing a letter containing this information to the Secretary of Tribunals. It is much safer, however, to use the standard form IT1, which has questions to get all the necessary information from you. IT1 forms are generally available from jobcentres, unemployment benefit offices, employment offices, citizens advice bureaux and from trade union officials.

filling in form IT1

Most of the questions on form IT1 are relatively straightforward. The most important questions to be answered are questions 1, 7 and 12.

Question 1 asks you to state what is to be decided by the tribunal. It is important to state all the questions you want the tribunal to decide. For example, if you think you have been unfairly selected for redundancy on the ground of your sex and have not received a redundancy payment, you should put "whether I was unfairly dismissed, whether there was sex discrimination, whether I should have received redundancy payment" as the questions to be answered by the tribunal. It is not fatal to your claim, however, if you state the wrong question to be answered, because the tribunal has a discretion to amend this and to insert the correct question.

Question 7 relates to your length of employment. This is important because in many cases it is necessary to show a prescribed period of continuous employment before you qualify to claim. For example, in an unfair dismissal case, you must have had two years' continuous employment with that employer if he has fewer than 21 employees. For a firm with over 20 employees, the qualifying period depends on when you started to work there: if that was before 1 June 1985, the period is one year; if after 1 June 1985, you will have to have been employed there for two years before you can claim. From 1 June 1987, the qualifying period will be two years for everyone.

It is important to state the dates when 'employment began and ended' with accuracy. The date of starting may be obtained from your contract of employment or your written statement of terms and conditions of employment. The date your employment ended – in law, the 'effective date of termination' – may be more difficult to ascertain.

★ If the contract is terminated by notice properly given, the effective date of termination is the date on which the notice expires.
★ Where payment in lieu of notice is given, the date will be the date of the notice.
★ If summarily dismissed, the relevant date is the date of dismissal.
★ If the employee resigns, it is the date on which he leaves whether or not he gives notice.

If you are not sure, do not be deterred from claiming – just put an approximate date. (The employer has to verify the accuracy later on, so any incorrect information can be identified then.)

Question 12 requires you to set out the grounds for your application, 'giving full particulars'. This means that in a claim for unfair dismissal, for example, you must not simply state baldly "I was unfairly dismissed". You should set out the circumstances surrounding your dismissal, the reason for your dismissal and why you think your dismissal was unfair. If you fail to give 'full particulars', the employer may apply to the tribunal for, or the tribunal may of its own accord require, further particulars; if these are not produced, the tribunal can dismiss the application without a hearing.

Question 13 says "If you wish to state what in your opinion was the reason for your dismissal, please do so here". It is generally wiser to leave this blank.

Question 14 asks you to state which 'remedy' you would prefer if the tribunal decides that you have been unfairly dismissed: reinstatement or re-employment or compensation. There are set maximum amounts of compensation that can be awarded.

Reinstatement means being taken back to the same job and to be treated in all respects, including seniority, pay and pension rights, as though you had never been dismissed.

Re-engagement means being re-employed but not necessarily in the same job or under the same conditions and terms of employment. The new job, however, must be comparable and suitable and, as far as is reasonably practicable, as favourable as the previous position.

The choice is not binding on you. But if you think you might wish to be reinstated or re-engaged, you should state so on the form because, if you do not, the tribunal might decide not to order reinstatement or re-engagement.

If you feel unsure about some aspect of completing form IT1, you should seek advice from someone such as a union official or at a citizens advice bureau.

Take a copy of the completed form IT1 for yourself and send the original to the Central Office of the Industrial Tribunals.

time limits

Although it is important that the IT1 form is properly completed, it is also very important to complete it as soon as possible to ensure that a claim is made within the proper period, otherwise the claim might become time-barred. The relevant date for this purpose is when the Central Office receives form IT1. The time limits are as follows:

claim	*time limit for applying to tribunal*
unfair dismissal	3 months beginning with effective date of termination of employment
written statement of reasons for dismissal not received	3 months beginning with effective date of termination of employment
interim relief pending determination of complaint of unfair dismissal*	7 days immediately following effective date of termination of employment
failure to offer re-engagement where dismissal connected with lock-out, strike or other industrial action	6 months beginning with complainant's date of dismissal
for redundancy payment	6 months beginning with date on which employment ceased (can be written application to employer)
for remuneration under protective award (redundancy)	3 months beginning with date of failure to pay
for compensation where order made by tribunal under the Transfer of Undertakings Regulations	3 months beginning with date of tribunal's order
for pay equal to that of an employee of the opposite sex doing like or equivalent work or work of equal value*	any time while doing the job, or six months from termination of employment

discrimination on grounds of colour, race, nationality or sex	3 months beginning with date of the act of discrimination
written statement of terms of employment not received*	any time after 13 weeks of starting employment while still in the employment or if employment has ceased, 3 months beginning with date on which employment ceased
itemised pay statement not received*	any time while in the employment or 3 months beginning with date on which employment ceased
time off with pay for ante-natal care	3 months beginning with day of ante-natal care appointment
maternity pay not received	3 months from last day of 6-week period in which maternity pay was due
guarantee payments during short-time or lay-off	3 months beginning with day when payment was payable
time off for trade union duties or activities and for public duties	3 months from date of employer's failure to give time off or to pay remuneration
unreasonable exclusion or expulsion from trade union	6 months beginning with date of refusal or expulsion
on employer's insolvency when Secretary of State will not pay debts owing to employee (wages) or unpaid contributions to occupational pension scheme	3 months beginning with date of communication of Secretary of State's decision

In cases marked *, it is essential that an application is made within the prescribed period; in other cases, it is not necessarily fatal to your claim if it is made outside the period.

on unfair dismissal
An unfair dismissal application should be presented within 3 months. If, however, a complaint is presented within a reasonable time after the three-month period, provided the tribunal is satisfied that it was not 'reasonably practicable' for the complaint to be presented within the three-month period, it may allow a complaint made later to go forward. But, in practice, only when the applicant was unaware of the time limit and there was nothing to make him aware of it might it be considered not reasonably practicable to present a claim in time – and subject to the limitation that the claim must still be made within a further 'reasonable' time.

A practical problem arises where the grievance is being dealt with through an employer's disputes procedure, and the procedure lasts longer than three months from the effective date of termination. The mere fact of a pending internal appeal, by itself, is not sufficient to render it not reasonably practicable to present a complaint to the tribunal in time. If the employer asks the employee not to complain to a tribunal while going through internal procedures, it might be considered not reasonably practicable to present a claim to a tribunal. An employee in such a situation is then faced with the dilemma of making a complaint to a tribunal and risking jeopardising the internal appeal or relying on the internal appeal to the exclusion of a tribunal claim.

eligibility to claim
For a claim of unfair dismissal, you must

- be below normal retirement age
- have had at least one year's continuous employment with that employer (two years in some cases)
- have been working at least 16 hours a week (or 8 hours a week for more than five years with that employer)
- be ordinarily working in Great Britain, under a contract of employment.

the application

When the IT1 form is received by the Central Office, it is vetted to eliminate applications which the tribunals do not have jurisdiction to hear.

If the Central Office considers that the applicant is not qualified to claim, the form will be returned, explaining why. If the applicant writes back to the Central Office stating that he wishes his case to proceed nevertheless, the Secretary of the Tribunals then has no option but to register the claim. Such insistence, however, carries the risk that if it turns out that he has no case, for the reasons given by the Central Office, he may be penalised by being ordered to pay costs at the end of the tribunal hearing.

Where the Central Office allows a claim to go forward, the application is passed to the appropriate regional office of the tribunals. The case is registered, and given a number and this number should be quoted in all correspondence connected with the claim.

the respondent

After a case has been registered, a copy of the IT1 form is sent by post to the person against whom the claim is made – the respondent (in most cases, the employer). He is also sent a form to complete, called 'notice of appearance' (form IT3).

The respondent should scrutinise the IT1 to ensure that the details which the applicant has given are correct, checking, in particular, the grounds stated for the complaint (questions 1 and 12) and the dates of employment given (question 7).

A respondent is given only 14 days from the date of receiving a copy of the IT1 form to provide an answer (this is called 'enter an appearance'). If the employer envisages that his investigations are likely to take longer, he should inform the regional office as soon as possible by letter, and ask for an extension of the time limit, giving reasons for his request.

Most of the questions in the IT3 form are relatively straightforward.

Question 4(a) asks whether the applicant was dismissed. This may not be in dispute, but if the applicant did in fact resign, this should be stated.

Question 4(b) asks the reason for dismissal. To rebut an unfair dismissal claim, the employer must show that the reason for dismissal was one which the law recognises as valid – namely, insufficient capability or qualifications, or misconduct, redundancy, or that continued employment would involve contravention of a statute, or some other substantial reason to justify dismissal.

Question 5 asks the respondent to give 'sufficient particulars to show the grounds on which you intend to resist the application'. In an unfair dismissal case, these particulars should be consistent with any reasons given in a letter of dismissal: any inconsistency is likely to result in the inference that the dismissal was unfair. In addition, question 5 should be used to state a preliminary point such as whether the applicant is qualified to take up the case or whether the claim is time-barred. This is sometimes called 'pleading in the alternative'.

Whether or not the claim will be resisted, the form should be returned. If notice of appearance is not entered, the respondent will not be entitled in most cases to take any further part in the proceedings.

The completed IT3 form, signed by the respondent, should be returned to the regional office within 14 days. Provided there were reasonable grounds for delay, however, the tribunal would usually treat a late entry as an application for an extension of time.

notice of hearing

Soon after the IT3 form has been returned to the regional office, both parties will receive a notice of the hearing (form IT4).

The notice must give at least 14 days' notice of the hearing. Although in practice more is generally given, it will not be much longer, so that the claim can be dealt with as quickly as possible. The tribunal has a considerable degree of discretion to postpone the day or time fixed for the hearing.

The hearing usually takes place at the regional office with which the parties have been corresponding. Where this is very inconvenient for one or both, they may apply to the regional office for the hearing to be held at a more convenient hearing centre. The regional office will not make a change without consulting the other party, who is given the opportunity to state whether the change would be convenient.

conciliation

From the outset of the claim (except for redundancy payment claims), copies of all the correspondence passing between the parties and the regional office of the tribunals will be sent to the regional office of the Advisory, Conciliation and Arbitration Service (ACAS). This correspondence is passed to a conciliation officer, who has a statutory duty in most cases to seek to promote a settlement of a complaint – for example, by an employee that he has been unfairly dismissed or discriminated against – without the dispute having to go to a tribunal hearing. The conciliation officer can be invited to step into the dispute by either party. Even if such an invitation is not made, however, the conciliation officer can act provided he considers that he would have a reasonable prospect of success.

The conciliation officer makes an initial approach to the employer and to the claimant separately, describes his role and offers his services to them. With a view to promoting a settlement and bringing the parties together, the officer will try to ascertain the background facts and the attitude of the parties.

Communications with a conciliation officer are 'privileged', which means that nothing said or shown to the officer can be used in evidence in the proceedings unless the person who made the communication consents. But the conciliation officer may tell one party what the other party has said unless something was said specifically in confidence.

The conciliation officer should be listened to carefully, because he has considerable experience of the law and of promoting settlements. But you are under no obligation to accept any offer of settlement made by the other side through the conciliation officer; there is no need to feel that an offer has particular authority just because it is the conciliation officer who puts it to you. Nor is it for the officer to adjudicate upon the merits of the case or any proposed settlement. He is not an arbitrator.

Should the conciliation work, however, it is important to make a settlement which is binding on both parties. The law is that any provision or an agreement to stop a person presenting a complaint to a tribunal, or bringing any proceedings, is normally void. But an exception is that a settlement is binding where it is reached through the good offices of a conciliation officer. A binding agreement can be made by both parties signing a form (COT3) which sets out the agreement which the parties have made; an agreement reached orally can also be binding. The agreement can then be recorded at the tribunal as a complaint settled by conciliation.

Before agreeing to a settlement, it is a good idea to discuss your options with someone such as a trade union official or an impartial adviser – for example, at a CAB or law centre. The conciliation officer has a duty to try to promote a settlement without recourse to a tribunal whereas, if you have a strong case, you might do better by taking your case to the tribunal.

preparing your case

A tribunal hearing requires a considerable degree of preparation on your part. Both parties have to place all the evidence before the tribunal and may also make submissions on the relevant points of law. Although you may get some guidance and encouragement from the tribunal when presenting your case at the hearing, a tribunal cannot be expected to know facts which have not been put to it in evidence.

You should be aware of the basic law which affects your case. The law can be found in statutes and judicial decisions. Perhaps the best starting point is to obtain the relevant free leaflet(s) on employment legislation issued by the Department of Employment. Some employment law textbooks may be in your local reference libraries. The most important tribunal decisions are collected in the Industrial Relations Law Reports, but these may be more difficult to obtain. If, at the hearing, your opponent relies on a case in the IRLR, you should ask the tribunal chairman to provide you with a copy of the report.

The citizens advice bureau may be able to guide you on the relevant reading in your case and help you to understand it.

There is a questionnaire procedure for cases under the Race Relations Act and the Sex Discrimination Act to help people who consider they have been discriminated against to decide whether to institute proceedings and, if they do, to formulate and present their case in the most effective manner.

further particulars

You should not come to a tribunal hearing without knowing the basis of your opponent's case. The IT1 and IT3 forms will generally state the basis of the claims of each party, but if these fail to give you the information you require, you should request 'further particulars' of what the other party's case is based on and 'any facts and contentions relevant thereto'.

You can request further particulars by simply writing a letter to your opponent setting out the specific information which you require of him – for example, asking for dates and description of alleged misconduct. It is advisable to send a copy of this letter to the regional industrial tribunal office.

You should set a time limit for compliance with the request. If the request is not complied with in full, an application can be made to the regional office for an order to require your opponent to provide you with the relevant particulars. You have to state the reasons why the information is needed.

If such an order is made against you and you are unhappy about it, you may apply to the tribunal, before the time for compliance, to have the order set aside or varied.

If an order for further particulars is not complied with, the tribunal may dismiss the whole or part of the originating application or strike out all or part of the notice of appearance or, after a warning has been given, direct that the respondent be debarred from defending altogether.

A tribunal may, on its own initiative, order either party to give further particulars.

documentary evidence

A crucial part of a case is likely to be the documentary evidence, so it is important to ensure that you have all the relevant documents in your possession before the hearing.

The documents which you will require depend on the particular case. For example, in an unfair dismissal case, the principal documents which an employee would want to have are

- his letter of appointment
- his contract of employment or written particulars of his main terms and conditions of employment

- the employer's disciplinary rules and procedures
- any previous written warnings
- minutes of any disciplinary hearing
- record of previous enforcements of a company rule
- letter of dismissal and a written statement of the reasons for dismissal.

An ex-employee with six months' continuous service has the right to ask his employer to set out the reasons for dismissal in a written statement. The employer must do so within 14 days of receiving the request and if the request is unreasonably refused or the reasons given are inadequate or untrue, the employee may have grounds for another claim to the tribunal.

An employer on his part is likely to be in possession of most of the information he requires from the outset, but he may wish to see job applications the claimant has made or details of unemployment benefit he has received, for the purposes of assessing compensation.

disclosing documents

If you find that you are not in possession of any documents you require, you should request them from your opponent. This can be done simply by sending a letter to your opponent, with a copy to the regional office, requesting the relevant documents and setting the time limit for compliance. It is also advisable to indicate your willingness to cooperate with your opponent by disclosing to him the documentary evidence on which you will rely.

If your opponent ignores or refuses to comply with your request, the tribunal has discretion to make an order for 'discovery' – this means providing a list of the documents he intends to refer to in support of his case. When you apply to the regional office for an order for discovery or inspection of the specific documents required, you should give reasons why you are requesting disclosure of the information. The other side can object to the disclosure order or ask to have it varied, but failure to comply with the order without reasonable excuse may result in a fine.

Problems may arise, especially in sex and racial discrimination cases, where confidential information is involved. The type of information which may be regarded as confidential includes company reports on employee performance, interview notes and the qualifications and experience of other applicants for the job. A tribunal faced with an application for disclosure of a specific confidential document will decide whether or not the information is necessary to dispose fairly of the case. If it is, the tribunal will order discovery but will generally seek to preserve confidentiality as far as possible – for instance in interview notes, blacking out such parts of the notes as are not necessary for the case and, where possible, replacing actual names by fictitious ones.

The tribunal may, on its own initiative, order the parties to bring documents to the hearing or to disclose them to the other side.

Make sure you have all your documentary evidence adequately prepared for the tribunal. Proper presentation saves time during the hearing and allows the tribunal members to focus their attention on the real issues in dispute. The documents, preferably numbered, should be in the order in which you will use them during the case. Take sufficient copies of the documents for each tribunal member and your opponent.

witnesses

Witnesses can be very valuable and you should seriously consider their use. Oral evidence by a witness is likely to carry greater weight with a tribunal than a written statement made by the witness, especially if it is on an issue where the evidence is contradictory.

You should only include witnesses whose testimony is likely to be relevant to the issue in dispute. Check in advance what the witness actually knows about the issue and also consider his truthfulness, how he will react to cross-examination, and his likely impression on the tribunal. You should prepare in advance a list of questions which you wish to ask him at the tribunal hearing (but you should not coach him on his answers).

If a witness is unwilling to attend the hearing, you may apply for an order (under rule 4) to compel his attendance. Such a course of action should be used cautiously, because a non-voluntary witness can be hostile and not helpful to your case. But an order for a witness to attend can be useful where a fellow employee is unwilling to testify because of fear of victimisation by his employer or where an employee cannot get time off with pay without a tribunal order.

If it is impossible for a witness to be free to attend the hearing and the evidence appears to be necessary, the tribunal can be asked to postpone the hearing until a date when the witness is available.

written representation

If, for some reason, it is not possible for a witness to attend, or his evidence relates to a matter not in dispute, a written representation may be used. The representation does not have to be in any particular form, but more weight will be given to an affidavit – that is a signed statement by the witness, who swears to the truthfulness of his statement before a person who is empowered to administer oaths (for example, a solicitor).

In the affidavit, the witness should identify himself and state what he would have said in oral evidence. For example, if the applicant was dismissed for fighting and claimed he was only acting in self-defence, the statement would amount to an eye-witness account of how the fight started, what happened next, and so on.

A copy of the written representation must be sent to your opponent and to the regional office at least seven days before the tribunal hearing. In Scotland, the written representation procedure is normally only regarded as appropriate where the facts are not in dispute or where the case is one which may be disposed of by way of submissions or argument only.

withdrawing the application

In the course of preparing his case, it may become apparent to the applicant that his claim is unlikely to succeed, or that he is not qualified to bring a claim. In such a case, the best course of action is to write to the regional office, withdrawing the application. This will result in the tribunal dismissing the claim.

If you proceed with a hopeless claim, an order for costs may be made against you.

the hearings

There are three types of hearing which may take place before the full hearing itself: pre-hearing assessment (PHA), preliminary hearing, interim relief hearing.

pre-hearing assessment

This stage in the proceedings was introduced with the idea of getting rid of unmeritorious claims at an early stage. Either party may apply to the tribunal for a pre-hearing assessment, but the tribunal is not obliged to hold one. A pre-hearing assessment may also be held at the tribunal's own initiative.

If the tribunal decides to hold a pre-hearing assessment, it will notify both parties, giving them an opportunity to submit representations in writing and to put forward oral argument at the hearing. No evidence from witnesses will be heard.

After considering the contents of the originating application, the notice of appearance, any representations in writing which have been submitted and any oral argument advanced by or on behalf of the parties, the tribunal may give an opinion that the application appears to have no reasonable prospect of success. It may then issue a warning that if the originating application is not withdrawn, the applicant may have an order for costs made against him after the full hearing.

Notwithstanding the tribunal's opinion, an applicant is entitled to proceed with the claim. If he does so, the full hearing will be heard by a tribunal consisting of different members, who should not be made aware of the opinions expressed at the pre-hearing assessment until after their own decision. But since continuing a case in these circumstances runs the risk of being penalised by an order to pay costs, it would be unwise to do so without specialist advice.

There have, however, been cases where applicants have won their case at the full hearing despite the opinion of the tribunal at the pre-hearing assessment that the application was unlikely to succeed (and vice versa). This has given rise to some disquiet about the role of the pre-hearing assessment in employment disputes and there are proposals for amending the procedure. Even so, it is very important that a pre-hearing assessment be treated seriously and proper preparation made, because it can have a significant bearing on the outcome.

preliminary hearing

A preliminary hearing will be called if it has to be decided whether the applicant is qualified to bring a claim. The tribunal itself may set the case down for a preliminary hearing.

If the respondent is of the opinion that there is a preliminary point to be discussed, such as whether or not the applicant has had sufficient length of continuous employment, he should write to the regional office asking for a preliminary hearing 'only'. The hearing will then be concerned only with evidence and argument relating to the preliminary point.

The parties are not under any legal obligation to attend a preliminary hearing, but it would be foolhardy not to go. From the applicant's point of view, if he loses the preliminary point when it is a qualifying point for unfair dismissal, then he will lose his whole case. So, the applicant should certainly attend, whether he is legally represented or not. From the employer's point of view, he may be well advised to attend, too, because the preliminary point may be the basis of his claim. He may be arguing that the applicant is not appropriately qualified to make a claim, and if he loses that point, he would have to concede that the dismissal was unfair. The onus is on the applicant to establish the competency of the claim.

If the preliminary point is decided against the applicant, the whole case will be dismissed. But if the preliminary point is decided against the respondent, the case will generally proceed to a full hearing.

Instead of holding a preliminary hearing, the tribunal may decide to hear the preliminary point first at the full hearing.

interim relief hearing

An applicant who considers the principal reason for his dismissal to be trade union membership or participation in trade union activities (or his refusal to join a particular trade union) can bring a claim for interim relief to a tribunal. This must be done within seven days from the date of dismissal. The application for an interim relief hearing has to be made on form IT1.

Where the applicant maintains that he was dismissed because of membership of or activity in an independent trade union, a certificate signed by an 'authorised official' of the union concerned must be sent to the central office of the industrial tribunals along with the IT1 form.

This certificate must state that the applicant was a member of the trade union and that there appear to be reasonable grounds for supposing that the dismissal was for the reason claimed by the applicant.

The hearing may be before a chairman sitting alone. If the employee can show that the reason for dismissal is likely to be held inadmissible, the tribunal can order his reinstatement or re-engagement. If the employer refuses to comply, he can be ordered to make payment to the employee, and, pending the full hearing, the applicant retains his employee status.

procedure for 'equal value' claims

Before 1984, women in employment could make a claim for equal pay only in respect of 'like work' (work of the same or broadly similar nature to that of a man) or work which had been rated as equivalent under a job evaluation scheme. But many employers do not carry out job evaluation schemes; also, the 'like work' standard is restrictive. The Equal Pay Act has been amended now to allow 'equal value' claims to include women doing work different from that of a man but which is of equal value to the man's work.

The procedural regulations for equal value claims are very complex and are contained in Schedule 2 to the Industrial Tribunal (Rules of Procedure) Regulations. The Department of Employment has published a free explanatory booklet *A guide to the Equal Pay Act*.

The initial complaint to the tribunal is made via the IT1 form and the notice of appearance made on form IT3. The principal difference to other claims is that there are three preliminary stages which are unique to the equal value claim.

● The tribunal must decide whether the case can succeed under the 'like work' provisions or if the woman's job and the man's have been compared under a valid job evaluation scheme.

● The tribunal may dismiss the case if it is satisfied that there are no reasonable grounds for determining that the jobs are of equal value. If it does not dismiss the case, it will invite the parties to apply for an adjournment to seek a settlement.

- The tribunal has a discretion, on the application of one of the parties, to consider the 'material factor' defence – namely, that the difference in pay is justified by a factor other than the difference in sex. An applicant should therefore come to a tribunal prepared, if necessary, to deal with the defence before the substantive merits of the case itself.

If these three hurdles are overcome, the tribunal must refer an equal value case to an independent expert, from a panel of people with experience in industrial relationships, appointed by ACAS. The obligations of the expert are basically to compare, after due consultation with the parties, the value of the applicant's job with that of her male counterpart. Once the expert completes a report, he or she sends it to the tribunal. The tribunal sends a copy of the report to the parties and fixes a date for the hearing.

At the hearing, the expert can be cross-examined on the report and either party may ask to be allowed to call one alternative expert witness to give evidence on the relative values of the jobs being compared.

The tribunal must determine whether to accept the expert's conclusion on the equal value issue. It can then consider a 'material factor' defence. There are therefore two opportunities for this defence to be considered.

The complexity of these new regulations should not discourage women from taking their case to a tribunal, but specialist advice should be taken before contemplating such an action.

the full hearing

Tribunals are open to the public and it is sensible to go and watch one before you have to attend your own.

For your own case, make sure that you take with you all relevant documents, and a pen and paper. Get there in plenty of time and be prepared to wait. The parties (and their witnesses) have separate waiting rooms.

If either party fails to appear at the hearing, the tribunal has discretion to adjourn, dispose of or dismiss the claim. In practice, if an applicant fails to appear, the tribunal is likely to adjourn and give him or her an opportunity to show good cause (in writing) for the non-appearance, rather than dismiss the claim.

Tribunals are specifically directed 'so far as appears appropriate' to avoid formality in their proceedings. In practice, the degree of informality and the procedure adopted depends, to a large extent, on the particular tribunal chairman. Some chairmen go out of their way to assist an unrepresented party to bring out the points material to his or her claim and may suggest questions to ask witnesses. A chairman has to take note of all points of law, whether or not they are raised by a party, and may seem unsympathetic because he draws attention to legal obstacles.

the procedure

Usually the tribunal chairman opens the case by making a few preliminary remarks about the procedure to be followed. The general rule is that whoever has to prove his case starts; in a case of unfair dismissal, it is usually the employer who starts (unless the dismissal is denied rather than its unfairness).

Whenever you are addressing the tribunal, you should speak slowly and distinctly, because the chairman will be taking notes, usually in longhand, of what you are saying.

You, too, should make notes of what is said, by the opposition and by witnesses, so that you can take matters up. You may be nervous and confused, so do not rely on your memory. Sometimes industrial tribunals go on longer than one day and the second day of a hearing may be separated from the first by a period of time, and your notes will then be vital.

The employer may start by making an opening statement, which sets out the background and summarises his case. There does not have to be an opening statement, however, and, in many cases, the tribunal prefers the employer to go straight into proving his case. (It is not the practice in Scotland to make an opening speech and the main regulations governing procedure now provide no entitlement for such speeches although the tribunal may permit an opening speech for the purpose of, say, clarifying an ambiguous statement in an application.)

witnesses

In Scotland, witnesses remain outside the tribunal room until called to give evidence.

Evidence is usually given on oath or affirmation. (The tribunal cannot compel a witness to take the oath but refusal may be taken into account in assessing the value of the evidence.)

The employer calls his witnesses and puts to them the questions he has prepared. He should avoid asking leading questions, such as "Is it the case that . . . ?" The applicant is given the opportunity to cross-examine each witness, using where possible a prepared list of questions.

Remember, when cross-examining, that you are not participating in a televison drama and that there is no need to adopt an aggressive bullying approach. Be polite but firm.

The tribunal members may also question the witnesses and sometimes assist an unrepresented applicant or respondent in the difficult art of cross-examination. The purpose of the tribunal members' questioning is to help determine the facts, not to indicate bias in favour of one party or the other. Such questions may also serve to focus on the important or contentious issues.

The employer will then be given an opportunity to re-examine his witnesses, on points which have arisen in cross-examination.

Once the employer has called all his witnesses, the attention then shifts to the applicant. He may make an opening statement, but does not have to do so – and in most cases, it is unnecessary. The applicant then calls his witnesses, and the process of examination and cross-examination is gone through.

closing statement

Once that is completed, the applicant makes his closing statement to the tribunal, which should summarise his case. It is helpful to prepare this in advance. It should be kept short, reiterate the most important pieces of evidence and the facts most helpful to your case, refer the tribunal to the relevant law and conclude by saying why you think you have made out your case. After that is done, the employer makes his closing statement, which should follow the same pattern.

the decision

After hearing all the evidence and the closing statements, the tribunal generally retires to make its decision. This may take a matter of minutes but, in the majority of cases, the decision is made in about an hour or two. There is no need for the decision to be unanimous, although most are.

The tribunal may return to read its decision, with reasons, to the parties. Where the case is a complex one, the tribunal may 'reserve' its decision, which means that the decision will be made at a later date and will then be sent, by post, to the parties. The written reasons for the tribunal's decision will be given either in full or, in most cases, in summary form and sent to the parties.

Full written reasons will automatically be given, however, where the tribunal decision relates to one of the following matters:

* complaint of dismissal, action short of dismissal or selection for redundancy on the grounds of trade union membership or activities or non-membership of a union
* application for interim relief from someone alleging dismissal on the grounds of trade union activities or non-membership of a trade union
* complaint of unreasonable exclusion or expulsion from a trade union in a closed shop
* claim for equal pay
* complaint of sex discrimination
* complaint of racial discrimination.

In other cases, either party has the right to ask the tribunal to provide full written reasons. The request should be made orally at the hearing, or in writing within 21 days from the date on which the summary written reasons were sent. If the request is made at any other time, the tribunal can decide whether or not to provide full written reasons.

Look carefully through the decision, with its reasons, to see if there is a possibility of an application for review or appeal.

remedies, costs and expenses

If the finding is in favour of the applicant, the tribunal will decide what remedy to order.

In an unfair dismissal case, the remedies available are reinstatement, re-engagement or compensation, as laid down by statute. Financial compensation normally consists of two components, a basic award on a scale based on the factors of age, wage and length of continuous service, and an award (up to a prescribed maximum) to compensate the employee for loss of past and future earnings and fringe benefits, loss of pension rights, loss of employment protection rights, and for the manner of the dismissal if this makes it difficult to get a comparable job. For all of these, the claimant will need to produce some evidence such as a P45 form, payslips, unemployment benefit card. Because the applicant has a duty to 'mitigate' (that is, reduce) his loss, he may be asked to show what he has done about trying to get another job.

In a redundancy case, the appropriate statutory payment will be ordered.

In sex and racial discrimination cases, the applicant is more likely to get a declaration of his or her rights, and compensation.

In an equal pay case, up to two years' back pay can be awarded or, if your claim succeeds under the equal value provisions, back pay for two years or until 1 January 1984, whichever is the shorter period.

enforcement

The document you get confirming the tribunal's decision is accompanied by information on enforcement proceedings, where necessary.

In England, Wales and Northern Ireland, if a compensation award is not complied with (which is relatively rare), the tribunals themselves have no enforcement machinery. Instead, an application has to be made to the county court to enforce the decision for the sum awarded, as a debt.

If an order for reinstatement or re-engagement is not complied with, the only remedy available is to come back to the tribunal, which has power to award additional sums by way of compensation for the failure to reinstate.

In Scotland, the tribunals have power to enforce. If payment has not been received within 42 days, a request to enforce should be made to the Secretary of the Tribunals in Glasgow without further delay.

costs and expenses

Costs (in Scotland, expenses) are not normally awarded. A tribunal does, however, have a discretion to award costs where, in its opinion, a party has acted 'frivolously, vexatiously or otherwise unreasonably' (rule 11). Tribunals also have discretion to award costs in respect of postponements and adjournments. An application for costs should be made as soon as the tribunal has given its decision.

Until recently, tribunals have tended to exercise sparingly their discretion to award costs, and the sums awarded have tended to be low. But both these tendencies are changing. Previously, the words 'vexatiously' and 'frivolously' were interpreted narrowly, but the introduction of 'otherwise unreasonably' in rule 11 has widened the scope. Among other things, costs may now be awarded against the claimant where a case goes on to a hearing despite the tribunal's opinion to the contrary at a pre-hearing assessment.

There is provision, at the chairman's discretion, for payment of an expenses allowance in connection with attendance at an industrial tribunal. At the end of the hearing, expenses allowance forms should be requested from the clerk, completed and returned by post. Allowances can be claimed by both parties (loser as well as winner) and their witnesses for their travelling and subsistence costs, and loss of earnings – but not lawyers' fees. There are set rates of allowances, which are paid in due course by the Department of Employment out of public funds. But if you are ordered to pay the other party's costs, you may not get your own expenses paid.

reviews and appeals

A tribunal decision can be challenged either by applying for a review or by appealing.

An application for a review can be made at the hearing if the tribunal's decision is given then; if not, it should be made in writing to the Secretary of the Tribunals at the Central Office within 14 days after the date on which the decision was sent to the parties (The time limit may be extended if good reason can be shown.)

The application should state in full the grounds on which the review is sought. There are five grounds for asking for a review, which are set out in rule 10:

* the decision was wrongly made because of an error on the part of the tribunal staff at the regional office or the Central Office: for example, failure to inform a crucial witness of the hearing
* a party did not receive notice of the proceedings leading to the decision
* the decision was made in the absence of a party or person entitled to be heard
* new evidence has become available since the conclusion of the hearing, the existence of which could not have been reasonably known or foreseen. (This evidence must be credible and be such that it would have an important influence on the result.)
* the interests of justice require such a review. (This has been narrowly interpreted and mainly confined to cases where a party claims that he was not given a fair opportunity to present and argue his case.)

The application may be refused if the chairman is of the opinion that there is no reasonable prospect of success.

If the review is granted, it will be heard by the original tribunal, where practicable. The reviewing tribunal has the power to confirm, vary or revoke the original decision and, if revoking, to order a re-hearing.

appealing

The alternative to applying for a review is to appeal to the Employment Appeal Tribunal (EAT) in London (4 St James's Square, London SW1Y 4JU) or Edinburgh (11 Melville Crescent, Edinburgh EH3 7LU) to reverse the decision of the industrial tribunal.

An appeal can be made only on a point of law – except in cases of alleged unreasonable exclusion or expulsion from a trade union in a closed shop situation where an appeal may be made on a point of law or fact.

A tribunal decision will not be interfered with simply because the appeal tribunal would have taken a different view of the evidence. Instead, it must be shown

* that the tribunal misunderstood the law
  or
* that the decision was so unreasonable that no reasonable tribunal could have reached such a decision
  or
* that the tribunal considered the wrong evidence.

You can ask the EAT office to send you the necessary form of notice of appeal. Notes for guidance will be enclosed, and a warning that an appeal must be lodged within 42 days of the date on which the tribunal's full written reasons for its decision were sent to the parties. (But the EAT has discretion to grant an extension.)

Because an appeal is generally on a point of law, a lawyer's help should be sought in completing the notice of appeal and for representation at the hearing. Unlike a hearing at an industrial tribunal, legal aid is available for an appeal to the Employment Appeal Tribunal and an unrepresented appellant's or respondent's expenses connected with attending the EAT will not be paid.

social security appeal tribunal

The appeal tribunals allow a person to challenge a decision that he shall not receive a social security 'benefit' which he had claimed in the belief that he was entitled to it.

The entitlement to some social security benefits is based on sufficient national insurance contributions having been made, such as a claim for
* unemployment benefit
* sickness benefit
* invalidity benefit
* child's special allowance
* maternity benefits
* widows' benefits
* retirement pensions

Or the entitlement may be based on the claimant's circumstances (financial or physical) falling within the statutory requirements, such as a claim for
* child benefit
* guardian's allowance
* severe disablement allowance

Or entitlement may be based on the claimant having insufficient means (income and capital) in relation to necessary outgoings, such as a claim for
* supplementary benefit (and single payments)
* family income supplement (FIS)

Or entitlement may be based on a medical condition, such as a claim for
* industrial injuries benefits
* attendance allowance
* mobility allowance

The social security appeal tribunals deal with appeals against refusal of a claim or against the amount of payment of benefit in all cases except the 'medical condition' ones.

Appeals on some medical issues are dealt with by adjudicating medical authorities (medical boards) and medical appeal tribunals. Attendance allowance, including disputes about attendance conditions, is administered by the attendance allowance board.

Housing benefit is administered by local authorities and has its own review structure through housing benefit review boards.

the procedure

Since 1984, much of the procedure for appealing against decisions relating to the various benefits has been standardised. Some differences do remain between the treatment of the means-tested benefits (supplementary benefit and family income supplement) and the other national insurance benefits.

Page 146 illustrates the sequence with its distinct stages starting with the adjudication officer's decision, followed by a two-tier appeal system, first to a tribunal, and then from the tribunal to the social security commissioners.

the initial claim

For most social security benefits, there is an explanatory pamphlet issued by the Department of Health and Social Security (DHSS) or the Department of Employment, and most have a claim form at the back. When sending in this part of the form, it is wise to send a covering letter, with the date. Keep a copy of this letter so that, if your claim is lost, you have a record of when you made your claim.

The completed form is processed at the local DHSS office (or unemployment benefit office, as appropriate) and your entitlement, if any, is established by an 'adjudication officer'. He is nominally independent of the DHSS or the Department of Employment.

Make sure that you supply all the required information and evidence to the adjudication officer.

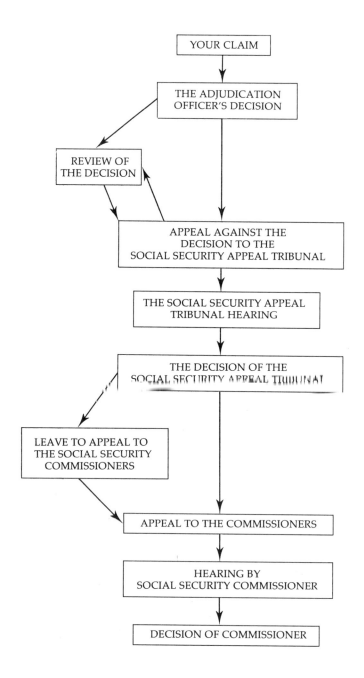

if there is delay

A delay on getting a decision on your claim may be caused by the papers being mislaid or just the volume of work at the local DHSS office.

If you are in financial hardship, ask for an urgent needs payment to tide you over while the claim is being settled.

If the delay is longer than 14 days from the date of your claim, you should

• check with the local office that the claim has been received and not mislaid;
• check that a decision is not being delayed because you have not provided enough information;
• complain to the manager of the local DHSS office – keep a copy of letters, and a record of any other communications and telephone calls. In cases of exceptional delay, complain to the Chief Adjudication Officer (Market Towers (Room 1306), 1 Nine Elms Lane, London SW8 5NQ).

Strictly, you cannot appeal until you have a decision, but you can try treating the delay as if it were a negative decision on your claim and write to the local DHSS office requesting an appeal to the appeal tribunal. This may have the effect of speedily resolving your claim one way or the other.

the adjudication officer's decision

If the adjudication officer's decision is unfavourable, reasons for the decision should be automatically given in all cases except those concerning supplementary benefit.

In a supplementary benefit claim, you have a right to a written statement of reasons if you apply for it within 28 days of the adjudication officer's decision. If the decision is that you are entitled to supplementary benefit or that you would be but for your other sources of income, an assessment of your entitlement is sent to you on form A14N. If the form A14N is incomprehensible, or you want greater detail as to how your benefit, or lack of it, has been calculated, ask for form A124 which gives a more detailed breakdown of the calculation. Although this can cause delay, if you intend to appeal against the decision, you should ask for form A124. A notice of refusal of a 'single payment' claim arrives with some indication why the payment has been refused.

On the written notification of the decision, you will be told of your right to appeal to an independent tribunal within 28 days of being given notice of the decision. If, in a supplementary benefit case, you have asked for written reasons for the decision, the 28-day period for an appeal starts to run from the date of being given the reasons.

The reasons for the decision may refer to 'the Regulations' governing entitlement to the benefit. The regulations give a legal entitlement to benefit if you fall within their provisions – as much an entitlement as if you were pursuing a debt that someone owed you.

The regulations are to be found, together with the relevant Acts of Parliament, in loose-leaf books published by HMSO:

• *The law relating to supplementary benefits and family income supplement* (referred to as the 'yellow book' because of the colour of its cover)

• *The law relating to social security and child benefit*, volumes I–IV (referred to as the 'brown books'), which include various non-means-tested benefits.

These books are constantly changing, especially the yellow book, and are updated by supplements. They can be inspected at the local office of the DHSS and may be available at your local library. Citizens advice bureaux also keep copies.

Finding your way round these regulations, particularly the supplementary benefit regulations, can be difficult. Even the adjudication officers are given guidance by the chief adjudication officer as to how to apply the regulations relating to supplementary benefits, through a publication called the *S Manual*, and through the issuing of 'S circulars' on particular points. The *S Manual* can be inspected at any local DHSS office and most CABx. It is only guidance as to how the regulations should be interpreted, but it does provide you with some ammunition when you are contesting the adjudication officer's decision if the decision appears to be contrary to the guidance expressed in the *S Manual*. A statement by an adjudication officer that "the Regulations do not allow for such a payment" or "you do not fall within the Regulations" may be refutable by "Regulation ... does cover my situation".

helpful reading

Useful information can be found in the
Child Poverty Action Group's publications:
The *National Welfare Benefits Handbook* (14th
edition 1985, £3.50)
covers rights regarding supplementary benefit,
family income supplement, health benefits,
housing benefit, education benefits.
The *Rights Guide to Non-means-tested Benefits* (7th edition 1985, £3.50)
covers unemployment, sickness, maternity and widows' benefits,
retirement pensions, death grant, benefits for people with severe
disabilities, benefits for children, industrial injuries benefit.

Both the *Handbook* and the *Guide* are updated in November of each
year, and can be obtained from CPAG, 1 Macklin Street, London
WC2B 5NH.

CPAG's *Supplementary Benefit Legislation Annotated* (2nd edition 1985,
published by Sweet & Maxwell, £13)
contains relevant annotated supplementary benefit and family income
supplement regulations, with explanatory comment referring to
reported and unreported decisions that could help your claim, as well
as parts of the *S Manual*. This book is virtually an annotated 'yellow
book'.

The *Penguin Guide to Supplementary Benefits* (5th edition 1985, £3.50)
is a full guide to the maze of supplementary benefit law.

The *Supplementary Benefits Handbook* (HMSO, 1984 edition £2.50)
is the official guide to the supplementary benefit scheme.

Disability Rights Handbook (1985 edition £2.20)
is a guide to rights, benefits and services for all people with disabilities.
It is published annually, with updating supplements (£1.50 each)
throughout the year, and is available from The Disability Alliance, 25
Denmark Street, London WC2H 9NJ.

review

If the adjudication officer's decision has gone against you, before appealing to the tribunal direct, you can ask the adjudication officer to review his decision. It is necessary to show that the adjudication officer had wrongly applied the relevant regulations, or was wrong for some other reason.

A request for a review can be made any time after the adjudication officer's decision. You should apply for a review in writing, stating the grounds why you want the decision reviewed. (The response is generally much quicker than waiting for a tribunal hearing.)

The adjudication officer has the power to review his decisions on the grounds that

* there was a mistake as to a material fact
* the original decision was made in ignorance of a material fact
* the circumstances have changed (not if a FIS claim)
* there was an error by the adjudication officer in interpreting the regulations – an error of law.

It is best to ask for a review on one of the first three grounds. You should state what mistake of fact was made or which fact was not known or what circumstances have changed. If this includes new evidence (medical, for example) it should be enclosed with your request for a review. If you just think that there was an error in applying the regulations and there are no new facts, it may be just as well to ignore the review stage and appeal against the decision to the tribunal direct, provided that you are still in time. An appeal from the original decision of the adjudication officer to the tribunal must be made within 28 days of notice of the decision being sent to you.

If you apply for a review and are unsuccessful, you will be given a new decision which you can appeal against. So, if you are outside the 28-day time limit for an appeal, you could try asking for a review of the decision and then if that review is unsuccessful, you have 28 days to appeal against the refusal to review the decision. The 28-day period starts from the date that notice is given of the refusal to review. (This provides an effective method of overcoming the problem of appealing if you are outside the statutory time limit.)

If you want to speed things up, you should write at the end of the request for a review "If this request is unsuccessful, please treat this letter as a letter of appeal".

getting advice

You should get advice as early as possible after the initial decision has been received. Even if you do not want legal representation, you can – and, in most cases, should – get advice on the law, and help with written submissions from an advice centre (or a solicitor under the 'green form' scheme if you are eligible).

Citizens advice bureaux and law centres can advise and assist you about all social security matters. They will have copies of the yellow book, and probably previous commissioners' decisions, and sometimes can arrange for someone to go to the tribunal with you. Even if you want to do the whole thing yourself, it is a good idea to discuss your options with someone who has had more experience in the field.

appeal to the social security appeal tribunal

You have to appeal against a decision taken by an adjudication officer within 28 days of being notified of the decision or the review. If you are outside the time limit, you should explain why you failed to appeal in time. The tribunal chairman can extend the time for appealing if he is satisfied that there are special reasons for doing so. There is no right of appeal from the chairman's decision on this point and he does not have to specify any grounds for his decision.

You should set out the grounds for your appeal in writing. These do not have to be too detailed, but the information you provide goes to the tribunal members before the hearing and is your opportunity to let the members know your grounds for the appeal. There is no need to use the official form provided by the DHSS (or the Department of Employment, where appropriate); a letter, or any written statement will do. You can send in further details later via the clerk to the tribunal if you are running out of time for lodging an appeal. Any new information you provide may prompt the adjudication officer to review the decision without the need for an appeal hearing.

The adjudication officer will, in any event, conduct a review following the lodging of an appeal. When you receive either the statement of reasons (in a supplementary benefit case) or the detailed submission and the decision turns out to have been soundly based, you may decide to withdraw.

The amounts of some benefit payments, such as the scale rates for supplementary benefit, are governed by regulations, and are not left to the adjudication officer to decide, so cannot be appealed against. Also, you cannot appeal against a decision on the method of payment of supplementary benefit, or for the replacement of lost girocheques.

being unrepresented

Most unrepresented claimants are apprehensive about appearing before a tribunal. But the object of proceedings before a social security appeal tribunal is to ensure that a claimant receives what (if anything) he is entitled to under the law, whether or not this accords with the contentions of the claimant or the adjudication officer.

The President of the Social Security Appeal Tribunals, Judge Byrt, has stated in the foreword to *Social Security Appeal Tribunals, a guide to procedure* that the unrepresented claimant

"of all people at the moment of an appeal will need help and guidance on how most effectively to present his appeal . . . most claimants at the time of their appeal will be too troubled and hassled by the more practical and day to day problems of their plight ever to have the emotional energy to study the nuts and bolts of the machinery by which their appeal will be processed . . . Let others, whose job it is to look after procedure, do so".

But claimants representing themselves are at a disadvantage in arguing the law and it is wise to get an experienced adviser to help you or even to represent you, perhaps via a citizens advice bureau. If you have to or want to present your case yourself, the tribunal should do what it can to help you with the law.

A claimant should not, however, rely on the tribunal to pick up new points which might be argued in his favour or to identify erroneous interpretations of the regulations by the adjudication officer.

Tribunals do not always get it right. A large number of tribunal decisions are overturned by social security commissioners when appealed against.

date of hearing

In your letter of appeal, you should state any dates when you are not available for a tribunal hearing.

You should be given at least 10 days' notice of the date, time and place of the tribunal hearing. The 10 days is calculated from the day the notice is given and ends on the day before the hearing. If sufficient notice has not been given, the tribunal cannot proceed without your consent.

If the date of the hearing is inconvenient for some reason, or you need more time to gather more evidence from a doctor, social worker, housing officer or other source, you should contact the clerk to the tribunal as soon as possible to try to obtain a different date for your hearing. This can normally be done on the telephone, followed by a written request confirming the reason for the postponement.

the appeal papers

Included with the notification of the hearing, you will receive a set of appeal papers. On looking at these papers, you may be tempted to call it a day. Do not be put off too much by the jargon in which they are written and the references to 'The Regulations' and items like 'R(S) 2/80', used by the adjudication officer to support his decision not to allow your claim.

The appeal papers (form AT2) will be typed and will state:

- the adjudication officer's decision
- what the adjudication officer believes to be the relevant provisions in the Acts and regulations which apply to your case, with appropriate references to the pages of the yellow book or brown books
- what the adjudication officer believes to be the relevant reported decisions of the social security commissioners (reported decisions of the commissioners are decisions with which at least a majority of the commissioners agree and which are published by HMSO).

Decisions which are reported bear the prefix 'R', followed by letters which indicate the benefit the decision was about:

  (A) decisions on attendance allowance
  (F) decisions on child benefit
 (FIS) decisions on family income supplement
  (G) decisions on maternity benefits, widow's benefits, guardian's allowance, child's special allowance, death grant

(I) decisions on industrial injuries benefits
(M) decisions on mobility allowance
(P) decisions on retirement pensions
(S) decisions on sickness and invalidity benefits and severe disablement allowance
(SB) decisions on supplementary benefit
(U) decisions on unemployment benefit

For example, 'R(SB)3/82' indicates that this is the third reported decision in 1982 on supplementary benefit. The appeal papers should indicate which paragraphs of the commissioners' decision the adjudication officer is relying on.

- your written grounds for the appeal
- a statement (called a submission) by the adjudication officer containing

★ the facts of the case, as known by the adjudication officer
★ the reasons for the adjudication officer's decision and the regulations and commissioners' decisions being applied to the facts of your case.

This is the case that the adjudication officer will present at the tribunal hearing, sometimes word for word.

If, after studying the papers carefully, you are still unable to understand why it is that the adjudication officer has given what you consider to be a wrong decision, do not give up, but seek advice from a citizens advice bureau or a law centre.

preparing your case

The tribunal will use the appeal papers as their starting point and so should you, bearing in mind that the tribunal are bound by the same statutory provisions, regulations and commissioners' decisions as the adjudication officer.

Commissioners' reported decisions are available for inspection at the local DHSS office, as is a digest of the main decisions, called *Neligan's Digest*, which may also be found in some reference libraries. The CPAG's *Welfare Rights Bulletins* summarise recent decisions – you can go to your citizens advice bureau to read them up.

Analyse the appeal papers with these questions in mind:

• Is the statement of the "Facts before the adjudication officer" correct? The chairman may ask you this question near the beginning of the tribunal hearing.

• Even if the facts are correct, are they misleading in that something important has been left out? If so, make a note of this and say so at the tribunal.

• Are any of the 'facts' really statements of opinion which you would wish to contest?

• Are some of the 'facts' based on reports made by officers, such as a DHSS visiting officer?
The officer is unlikely to be present at the tribunal to confirm his evidence and his report is not available to you. You may therefore want to ask for the report to be made available or for that officer to be present so that you can ask him questions about his report. Such a request should be made to the tribunal clerk in advance of the hearing, wherever practicable, since doing this may save the need for an adjournment. Where this is not practicable, the request can be considered at the hearing by the tribunal who have a discretion as to whether they will require the presence of the witness.

• In the "Reasons for the adjudication officer's decision", you should try to check that the regulations are correctly cited. Sometimes an adjudication officer puts into this section only the parts of the regulations that are specifically detrimental to your case. You need to check that parts of regulations have not been omitted that could help your case, and whether there are other regulations that would support your case.

• Where the regulations are correctly cited, is it possible to interpret the sentence or phrase relied upon by the adjudication officer in a way that is more favourable to your case? For example, on supplementary benefit, a commissioner's decision has declared that

> "The supplementary benefit legislation is directed to satisfying the requirements of claimants, and the approach must broadly be subjective rather than objective, although, of course, it cannot be pursued to such absurd lengths that personal idiosyncrasies are catered for to the exclusion of all objective criteria based on reasonableness." (from paragraph 5 of R(SB)1/84)

This means that, where possible, the tribunal should construe the regulations with regard to the particular needs of the claimant, wherever the regulations allow. In practice, the regulations normally clearly define the circumstances that can be taken into account. Nevertheless, try to interpret the regulations so that they support your case if possible.

The relevant commissioners' decisions that have been cited by the adjudication officer might be totally inappropriate to the special facts of your case, or there may be other decisions which are more favourable to your case that have not been included.

gathering evidence

Having worked through the appeal papers in this way, you can plan the arguments that you are going to put to the tribunal, where possible using the statutory provisions, regulations and extracts from commissioners' decisions to support your lines of attack. It would be advisable to write out a plan to take to the tribunal so that you make sure that you do not forget anything.

There may be more that you can do. You should get together any evidence that can support your case, such as medical reports, job interviews, evidence of income, witnesses who may help to confirm your actions or give expert evidence (social workers, housing officer, fellow employees), estimates that particular items cost more where you live than the DHSS are prepared to give for a single payment.

If you are going to use witnesses or are asking for written evidence, make sure that you tell the person concerned the purpose of the evidence. If a witness cannot, or will not, appear in person, there is no method of forcing him to do so by issuing a witness summons. However, try to get a sworn statement of his evidence.

If you intend to produce any document at the hearing you should, if possible, send the tribunal clerk a copy of the document a few days before the hearing, so that he can have copies made for the members of the tribunal and the adjudication officer. If you cannot do this before the tribunal hearing, bring with you copies of any relevant documents, including copies of commissioners' decisions if you have been able to get hold of them, for each of the tribunal members (three copies) and for the adjudication officer.

If you were suddenly to produce new evidence at a tribunal hearing, the adjudication officer could ask for an adjournment at the hearing itself. But it is preferable to produce such evidence at the hearing than not to produce it at all for fear of an adjournment.

the tribunal hearing

If you do not turn up for the hearing, the tribunal will give such directions as they think proper with regard to all the circumstances, including any explanation that you may have offered for your absence. They can adjourn the hearing so that you can attend, or continue and reach a decision without your presence.

The tribunal should first of all have checked with the tribunal clerk to make sure that you were given proper notification of the hearing. The regulations require the posting of the notice of the hearing to the ordinary or last known address (it is immaterial whether you actually received the notification). If this cannot be established, the proceedings should be adjourned.

going to the hearing

It is important that you go along to the appeal hearing; if you have any misgivings, take along a friend, neighbour or relative for moral support.

Things to take with you include

* money for fares
* tribunal papers
* written summary of your arguments
* books and papers relating to the law in question
* two pens (in case one runs out) and paper for taking notes.

It would be worth reading, or re-reading, *Social Security Appeal Tribunals, a guide to procedure* (HMSO £2.50) an explanatory booklet for tribunal chairmen and members, for claimants' representatives and for unrepresented claimants.

The tribunal's independence should be reflected by its physical location. Where a tribunal is held on premises that you may associate with the DHSS, the actual tribunal room should be physically separated from any DHSS work taking place in the same building. Tribunals can take place in the town hall, trade union meeting room, and even a youth club.

the clerk

The clerk performs the clerical work of the tribunal, sending the papers out, and ensuring that copies of the relevant materials are available to the tribunal at the hearing. It is the clerk you will need to contact about adjournments, getting papers to the tribunal in advance, and practical matters such as facilities for a disabled person.

The clerk may also be able to help if you are having difficulties getting hold of any of the material you need to prepare your case (such as yellow and brown books, commissioners' decisions).

The clerk can be asked to explain any of the procedure that you are unsure about.

expenses

When you get there, you will meet the clerk to the tribunal and will be asked if you incurred any travel expenses. Either the clerk will complete an expenses form for you and ask you to sign it, or you will be asked to complete the form yourself. Clerks have a cash float and you can ask for the money to be paid immediately, or you can send in your claim later.

Provided you ask the clerk in time, you can get the expenses in advance, or a travel warrant. You can also claim for the expenses of witnesses or of someone else who had to come to the hearing to help you for any reason.

Normally, the expenses allowed are for travel by public transport or a mileage rate if you travelled by car. Taxi fares can be refunded only if the department's doctor or the tribunal chairman agrees that you needed to travel by taxi because of your health or because there is no suitable public transport.

You can claim a subsistence allowance if you are away from home or work for at least $2\frac{1}{2}$ hours. There is also provision for childminding expenses. If you are near the end of the morning or afternoon list of appeals to be heard, and all the claimants have turned up, you could be in for a long wait because although you have been given a set time for your appeal, the cases before you may well take longer than anticipated.

You can also claim for lost earnings, but there is a maximum amount allowed. You will have to provide a statement, with your employer's official stamp, of how much you earn an hour, and of how much money you expect to lose. If you are self-employed, you just write 'self-employed' on the form and work out how much you have lost by attending; there is still a maximum rate.

the tribunal

One way of helping to overcome your apprehensions is to attend somebody else's tribunal hearing, either on a different day or while you are waiting for your case to come up, so that you can get some idea of the procedure. Tribunals are public hearings and any member of the public can attend unless

* the claimant requests the hearing to be in private, or
* the chairman considers that intimate personal or financial circumstances of the claimant may have to be disclosed, or
* the chairman considers that considerations of public security are involved.

When your appeal comes up, you can ask the chairman for a private hearing if you want to. Although there are not normally queues of people wanting to attend tribunal cases, sometimes there is an advice centre worker or student observing how the tribunal is run, or a newly-appointed tribunal chairman or member and perhaps DHSS officials being trained.

who will be there?

The adjudication officer who is going to present the case should enter the room with you, not be already there talking to the tribunal.

the chairman

All chairmen of social security appeal tribunals appointed since 23 April 1984 must be legally qualified – that is, solicitors or barristers (or advocates in Scotland) of not less than 5 years' standing, appointed from a panel established by the Lord Chancellor (in Scotland, the Lord President of the Court of Session). There are transitional arrangements which allow any previously appointed chairmen who are not legally qualified to continue hearing supplementary benefit appeals until 23 April 1989.

The chairman sits in the middle and will introduce the other members of the panel to you, as well as the other people attending. He will then probably briefly explain the procedure that is to be followed, stressing the independence of the tribunal from the DHSS, the Department of Employment or any government department. In the *Guide to procedure*, he is advised to "ensure that the atmosphere of the hearing is friendly and encouraging".

the members

The two members sit on either side of the chairman. They will be drawn from a panel, established by the President of the Social Security Appeal Tribunals and Medical Appeal Tribunals, of people with knowledge or experience of conditions in the area. If practicable, at least one of the members should be the same sex as the claimant.

Remember throughout the whole hearing that, although the chairman may often appear to dominate the hearing, the members are just as much a part of the tribunal and, when both are present, can outvote the chairman. This does happen although it is not a common occurrence. So, do not just address yourself to the chairman (even if the other two seem to be less important).

medical assessor

If the appeal involves medical issues or evidence, a doctor may sit with the tribunal if the chairman considers that his professional knowledge would assist the tribunal. The medical assessor is not a member of the tribunal, nor is he a witness and he cannot be questioned by you, nor is he there to examine you physically; his function is only to help the tribunal on the medical points.

incomplete panel

If one of the members is absent, the appeal can continue, but only if the claimant signs his consent that the hearing can take place without a full tribunal. If the hearing does go ahead, the chairman has a casting vote.

If you feel that your claim might be affected, you should ask for the hearing to be postponed. It is difficult to assess whether to proceed or not in this situation. Having built up to the moment, you may well want to continue; also, a further delay might cause you further hardship.

On the other hand, you might decide to refuse to continue without a full tribunal panel where the appeal concerns supplementary benefit and revolves around a provision in which the local conditions are an important factor (for example, has there been a period of exceptionally severe weather? is there alternative furnished accommodation available in the area?). You might also consider refusing if you are trying to stretch a regulation to cover a commonsense situation where the benefit should be payable.

If a chairman or member of the tribunal discovers that they have a personal connection or a professional or work connection with you, as claimant, or your witnesses or the adjudication officer, they should consider whether or not to disqualify themselves from sitting on the tribunal panel. If the connection involves the chairman, the proceedings will have to be adjourned; if the connection involves a member and he therefore withdraws, it would be up to the claimant to decide whether or not to continue with a reduced tribunal panel.

If you think that there is some connection between yourself and a member of the tribunal which might affect your appeal, you should raise this immediately if the other interested party fails to do so. If the connection is remote (for example, a member lives in the same street as you, or is a teacher at your child's school), it may be that a general declaration of the interest will suffice, so long as you do not object to the member continuing to hear the case.

procedure at the hearing

The tribunal is bound by the same laws and regulations as the adjudication officer was when coming to his decision on your case. You need to convince the tribunal that you do fall within the appropriate regulation, or that there were facts which were not before the adjudication officer or which the adjudication officer overlooked or misinterpreted, which should give rise to a change in the original decision that was reached as to your benefit entitlement.

behaviour

During the hearing, if you are unsure about some part of the procedure or the regulations involved, ask the tribunal chairman to explain the matter to you. The tribunal must help you if you are in difficulties or are not sure what is going on, and you should not feel embarrassed to ask for help. Remember, they sit on tribunals regularly, while you are a stranger to the procedure.

The normal method of addressing the chairman is 'Mr chairman' or 'Madam chairman'. All comments should be addressed to the chairman and you should ask him or her when you want to put a question to the adjudication officer or his witness.

If you start to interrupt while the adjudication officer is presenting his case, the chairman will probably stop you and tell you to wait your turn. Similarly, if the adjudication officer tries to intervene while you are speaking and the chairman does not stop him, you should ask the chairman if you can finish what you were saying without interruption.

The chairman, especially a legally qualified chairman, may ask you to slow down at times because he will be trying to take notes of the proceedings. In which case, stop talking until you can see that he has finished writing or until he tells you to continue.

Chairmen are advised in the *Guide to procedure* to "let the claimant put any points he may wish to make in his own way and air any relevant real or imagined grievance, so that nobody can reasonably say that he did not have a fair hearing". A fair hearing where you can air your grievances does not, however, mean that you will win (although you may feel better after letting off some steam): you can only win by putting forward the facts and bringing yourself within the legal provisions.

the stages

The chairman is in control of the procedure adopted at the hearing; the basic stages of the hearing are

* introductory remarks by the chairman
* the adjudication officer presents his case and any witnesses
* the chairman asks if you agree with all the facts as stated in the appeal papers (form AT2)
* you can respond to the adjudication officer's case, including asking him and his witnesses questions
* the chairman asks you to present your case, including any witnesses
* the adjudication officer may respond to your arguments, as may the tribunal panel
* the chairman will close the proceedings after ensuring that all sides have completed their arguments. He may summarise the main points.

The sequence of these stages may vary. In particular, you may be asked to present your case first and you may be asked to confirm the facts on the AT2 at the beginning. If you are given the choice, it is usually better to let the adjudication officer presenting the case go first, so that you can hear the other side's arguments.

the adjudication officer presents his case

This will normally come straight from the written arguments presented in the appeal papers that were sent to you (form AT2). The adjudication officer presenting the case is often not the adjudication officer who gave the decision on your claim, or who prepared the appeal. Whether he is or not, he may sometimes depart from the written submission, even to the extent of finishing up supporting the appeal. Where the adjudication officer cites a statutory provision, regulation or commissioners' decision, he should offer to show you the relevant part from the yellow book or book of commissioners' decisions.

Make notes, if you can, particularly of what the presenting officer says. It is hard for trained personnel to recall what was said five minutes earlier – let alone a nervous claimant.

The chairman or members may intervene to clarify points. Do not jump in yourself – your turn will come later. If you disagree with something the adjudication officer has said, do not interrupt (that might just antagonise the chairman); make a note of it and raise it after the adjudication officer has put his case. If the adjudication officer brings any witnesses (which is unusual) and you disagree with them, again wait until the adjudication officer's case has finished; you will be given the opportunity to question both the adjudication officer and his witness.

the chairman asks you if you agree with the facts stated on form AT2

You should have checked the 'Facts before the adjudication officer' in advance and be prepared to question some items, if necessary – for example, dates, details of correspondence, omitted relevant facts. Sometimes assumptions by adjudication officers creep into the facts, and any statements of opinion which are not facts should be challenged.

the chairman asks you to respond

You can question the adjudication officer and any witness at this stage on any points that you may have disagreed with.

If the adjudication officer has raised points which were not on form AT2, or commissioners' decisions which you have not had the opportunity to look up because they were not cited on form AT2, you can ask for an adjournment of the appeal so that you can have a chance to gather evidence which may support you on these new points.

presenting your case
It is best to break down your case into various parts.

1. Start with a brief explanation of what the appeal is about in your own words.
2. Present the facts of the case in detail. This could start with a brief statement of your work or medical history. If you are out of work, a brief recount of what work you used to do and any attempts that you may be making to find work could provide a good background.
3. You should then go through the facts of the case, bring forward any witnesses that you have brought along, and present documentation to back up your version of the facts.
4. Apply the facts of your situation to specific regulations, illustrating how you can bring yourself within the statutory provisions. If appropriate, use relevant commissioners' decisions to help you.
5. Finish with a summary of your case.

While you are presenting your case, the adjudication officer should not intervene without the permission of the chairman. However, at any stage of the hearing, the chairman may intervene or allow a member to ask questions, of yourself, of your witness or of the adjudication officer. The chairman may also intervene to stop lengthy speeches which have little relevance to the appeal.

the adjudication officer responds to your case
The adjudication officer can respond to your case and ask you and your witnesses questions, as can the tribunal panel. If you wish to clarify something as a result of these questions, you should ask to be allowed to do so.

the chairman closes the proceedings
Once the chairman is satisfied that all sides have said what they want to say, he will close the proceedings. Claimants may be asked to wait behind for a short time, in case the tribunal want to put further questions to the adjudication officer or to the claimant.

After the tribunal have finished their deliberations at the end of the hearing, the chairman will tell you that you will receive a written decision not later than a week to ten days after the hearing (perhaps even earlier). In cases other than supplementary benefit appeals, you will probably be informed of the decision more or less straightaway, the formal written decision following by post later.

the decision of the tribunal

If the written decision has not arrived a week to ten days after the hearing, ring the clerk to the tribunal to find out what has happened.

The decision (sometimes handwritten, but you can ask for a typed copy) will be on form AT3 and consist of

- the chairman's notes of the evidence
- the findings of the tribunal on the questions of fact material to the decision
- the full text of the (unanimous or majority) decision on your appeal – this is where you will find out whether or not you have won – the tribunal will have
  - ★ allowed your appeal in full, or
  - ★ allowed your appeal in part only, or
  - ★ upheld the adjudication officer's decision
- the reasons for a dissent if the tribunal were not unanimous
- the reasons for the decision – this should include why the evidence was accepted or rejected, and identify the regulations or statutory provisions under which the award was or was not made.

If you have lost, do not throw away the form AT3 or tear it up in anger and frustration. You may be able to appeal, and will then need this document.

complaints procedure

If you are not happy about the way the tribunal had conducted your case in any way (for example, bias, too many interjections by the clerk, failure to hear your witnesses), whether or not you are appealing against the decision, you can complain to the President of the Social Security Appeal Tribunals and Medical Appeal Tribunals (Almack House, 26/28 King Street, London SW1Y 6RB). You can also complain to the Council on Tribunals.

The Council on Tribunals (St Dunstan's House, Fetter Lane, London EC4A 1BT) is a statutory body whose responsibilities include the receiving and investigating of complaints about the conduct of most tribunals.

appealing against the decision of the tribunal

If you have lost at the tribunal, all is not over. There are various options open to you. You can

- apply to have the decision set aside
- ask the adjudication officer to review the tribunal's decision
- accept the tribunal's findings and apply again later
- appeal to the social security commissioners.

These appeal options are also available to adjudication officers if you have won your case. You could find that, although the tribunal decision went in your favour, you receive a letter informing you that the adjudication officer is appealing or seeking leave to appeal against the tribunal's decision. In some cases, payment of the award made by the tribunal will be suspended pending the outcome of the adjudication officer's application. (If this does happen, you should consider applying to the DHSS for an urgent needs payment to tide you over this period if you are in financial difficulties.)

If you have not had any assistance from a law centre, CAB or other advice agency so far and you want to take your claim further, you would be well advised to seek help now.

setting aside
You can apply for a decision arrived at in your absence to be set aside (if it appears just to do so) in the following situations:

- where a document relating to the hearing at which the decision was taken was not sent to or received by a party to the proceedings or his representative
- where a document was not sent to or received by the tribunal
- where a party or his representative were not present at the hearing.

An application for a decision to be set aside should be made to your local office of the DHSS or the local unemployment benefit office. If this is refused, there is no easy method of challenging the refusal to set aside a decision. But you can apply for leave to appeal against the original tribunal decision on the grounds of a breach of the rules of natural justice.

When a tribunal decision is set aside it ceases to have effect and the original decision of the adjudication officer is reinstated, until the matter is reheard by a different tribunal.

adjudication officer's review
You can apply to the adjudication officer to review the decision of a tribunal on the following grounds

- that there was a mistake as to a material fact
- that the original decision was made in ignorance of a material fact
- that the circumstances have changed.

If the adjudication officer refuses to review the decision, you then have a new right of appeal to a tribunal and you can start all over again.

applying later
In a case such as a refusal of a single payment (for furniture and household equipment, for example), you can make a new claim later – when perhaps your circumstances have become even more acute or your circumstances are now such that a different regulation applies.

appeal to the social security commissioners

In many cases, the appeal from a tribunal decision is a two-stage process: before you can actually appeal to the commissioners, you need first to obtain leave to appeal.

You can appeal directly only if the decision of the tribunal is a majority one concerning a benefit other than supplementary benefit or family income supplement. (A majority decision is where one of the tribunal disagreed with the decision of the others.)

Leave to appeal is required in all supplementary benefit and family income supplement cases and after a unanimous decision concerning the other national insurance benefits.

You should seriously consider taking legal advice at the stage of appealing to the commissioners. If there is no law centre near you, your local citizens advice bureau may run a special legal advice session. You can also seek legal advice from any solicitor under the 'green form' scheme, if you are eligible, although in practice there are not many solicitors who are experts in this field. The CAB may be able to tell you of any in your area.

grounds for appeal

In supplementary benefit and family income supplement cases, you can appeal only if the decision is wrong because of an 'error of law'. In all other cases, there is a right of appeal if you think the tribunal got either the facts wrong or the law, or both.

Whether there has been an 'error of law' is sometimes difficult to assess and this is where an advice agency specialising in tribunal work would be able to advise you.

Generally, there is an error of law if the tribunal

* wrongly interpret the Act and the regulations
* fail to apply the correct law
* arrive at a decision which is not supported by any evidence
* take into account irrelevant matters or fail to consider relevant matters
* are in breach of the rules of natural justice
* do not give an adequate statement of the reasons for their decision. Reasons are not adequate where you are unable to tell from the decision
  – what has been decided
  – what the tribunal found were the facts of the case
  – what they thought the law was which was relevant to your case.

applying for leave to appeal

The time limits for applying for leave to appeal are rather confusing.

● In the first six weeks after the decision has been posted to you, you can apply to the chairman of the tribunal. If he refuses leave to appeal, you have a further six weeks from the notice of his refusal to apply for leave to a commissioner.

● After six weeks from the decision of the tribunal, applications for leave to appeal go direct to the commissioners and you have up to three months from the tribunal decision to make this application. If, therefore, you delay your application for longer than six weeks after the tribunal decision, you have no second chance.

Applications for leave to appeal go through the clerk to the tribunal. You should state in a letter your reasons for applying for leave to appeal, and send it to the clerk to the tribunal via the local DHSS office or the unemployment benefit office. Remember to keep a copy, because if you are successful in obtaining leave, you can use these reasons again to support the actual appeal to the commissioners.

In your application, try to get the reasons for seeking the appeal to fall into one of the categories that constitute an 'error of law'. Probably the one to concentrate on is that the reasons for the decision were not adequately stated.

In a case not concerned with supplementary benefit or family income supplement, you can point out that you are challenging the facts as found by the tribunal, and give your reasons why – for example, if at the hearing you questioned the facts as stated on the form AT2 and no reason is given in the written decision why the adjudication officer's version was preferred to yours, put this down as a ground for seeking an appeal. If some evidence was rejected, either documentary or the evidence of a witness, and the tribunal decision does not say why it was rejected, this can be a ground for appeal.

Basing an appeal on the natural justice ground alone is tricky. A failure of a member or the chairman to disqualify himself from hearing the case because of a professional or business or family relationship with yourself or with the adjudication officer could give rise to such a claim. If you are complaining about the conduct of the tribunal members, you must be specific in your complaint, such as failure to hear a witness or accept written evidence. An attack in general terms will not succeed. Remember that the tribunal has the right to intervene and ask you questions to clarify points, and this in itself is not evidence of any bias against you.

If you have pursued your application for leave to appeal to the commissioners and have been refused, this, in practice, is the end of the road and you have exhausted your possible avenues of appealing against the decision.

Once leave to appeal is granted, there are three months in which to make the appeal to the commissioners.

the appeal

The social security commissioners are an independent body of barristers or solicitors (advocates in Scotland) of at least 10 years' standing. They have two main functions:

● to consider applications for leave to appeal against the decision of a tribunal if the application is made more than six weeks after the tribunal decision. You can ask for the commissioners to hear your leave to appeal and your actual appeal at the same time.

● to consider appeals from the decision of tribunals and thus provide a second, albeit limited, chance of winning your case.

There is a right to appeal direct to the commissioners on a non-means-tested benefit claim where the tribunal decision was a majority not an unanimous one. This should be done within 3 months from the date the tribunal decision was posted to you. In all cases, the commissioners may extend the time limit if there are special reasons for doing so.

The clerk to the local tribunal will provide a form on which to make your appeal, and a pre-paid envelope. (If you have obtained leave to appeal to the commissioners, you can use the same reasons as you used in your application for leave to appeal.) After you have sent back the completed form, most of your correspondence will be with the office of the commissioners direct. The addresses are: 6 Grosvenor Gardens, London SW1W 0DH; 23 Melville Street, Edinburgh EH3 7PW; 16 Park Grove, Cardiff CF1 3BN.

Appeals to the commissioners take many months, some as long as two years. If the matter is urgent – for example, you have not got any money – ask the local DHSS office for an early hearing and send a copy of your letter to the office of the social security commissioners. (But consider also making an application to the DHSS for an urgent needs payment.)

oral hearing?

The form asks whether you want an oral hearing before a commissioner. If you say 'no', the commissioner can decide the case on the written material he has before him.

You may want an oral hearing in order to put forward issues of fact more clearly, or so that the commissioner can see your medical condition at first hand. If in doubt, say that you want an oral hearing – you can withdraw this request at a later stage. For your reason, put something like "it may help the commissioner to hear oral arguments".

The commissioner can refuse a request for an oral hearing, or can direct an oral hearing even where neither the claimant nor the adjudication officer has asked for one.

preliminaries

The adjudication officer will submit 'observations' to the commissioner. You will be asked if you wish to comment on these observations which you should do within the time allowed (you can ask for this period to be extended if there are reasons why you have failed to meet the time limit). If you have not already done so, you should at this stage go to an advice agency specialising in tribunal work, or a law centre.

The exchange of correspondence between the adjudication officer, the commissioner and yourself can continue for some time, with each side being offered the opportunity to comment on the other's observations at all times. At some stage, either you or the adjudication officer has got to call a halt to this flow of correspondence which will have left you with a bundle of case papers inches thick. Once you have said all you want to say, following the same pattern of argument as was used at the tribunal, tell the commissioner who will either arrange a date for an oral hearing if requested, or decide the matter on the basis of the case papers.

the commissioner's decision

Usually a case is heard by a single commissioner. Occasionally, where the issue is of some legal importance, three commissioners hear it; they are then called a 'tribunal of commissioners'.

If you have an oral hearing in front of the commissioner, be prepared for a far more formal court-like setting than at the tribunal. The adjudication officer may even be represented by a solicitor so, in order that you have a fair chance of putting your side of the case, you should try to get some advice from someone who has had experience of these type of hearings. But you cannot apply for legal aid to be represented by a lawyer at a hearing before commissioners.

In national insurance cases (non-means-tested), the commissioner will go through the whole case again – the facts at issue as well as the detailed interpretation of the regulations. If the adjudication officer has conceded any points in the written observations prior to the hearing, do not sit back and think that those points will not therefore be argued

at the hearing. They can be, because the hearing before the commissioner is a complete re-hearing, similar to the one you went through at the tribunal, to determine questions of both fact and law.
At the end of the hearing, the commissioner may

* decide the case himself, or
* refer the case to a differently constituted tribunal.

In a supplementary benefit or a family income supplement case, the only issue to be decided is the 'error of law' that you have successfully obtained leave to appeal against.

The commissioner has the power to hold that the decision of the tribunal was wrong on a point of law and

* give the decision the tribunal should have given, or
* refer the case to a differently constituted tribunal. This does not mean that you have won: you have to go through another tribunal hearing. But this tribunal will have been told to apply the law correctly or to hear the case in a proper manner.

There are restricted rights of appeal on a point of law to the Court of Appeal (Court of Session in Scotland) from the decisions of commissioners, but you would need legal help to pursue this course of action. Legal aid is available for appeals to the courts.

medical decisions

An 'industrial injuries' leaflet (NI.2) issued by the DHSS lists the prescribed diseases covered by the industrial injuries scheme, and describes briefly the benefits available and how to claim them. Leaflet NI.6 gives further information about disablement benefits, how to claim and rights of appeal. Severe disablement allowance is dealt with in leaflet NI.252, and leaflet NI.211 explains mobility allowance for people unable or virtually unable to walk, and includes an application form.

You can appeal to the 'adjudicating medical authority' (either a single doctor or two doctors sitting as a medical board) against an adjudication officer's decision on medical questions relating to severe disablement, mobility allowance, industrial injuries benefits and some decisions relating to prescribed industrial diseases.

The function of the adjudicating medical authority is to examine you medically and to decide on the medical point (such as the degree of disablement), and no more. You have no right of representation, but you can have someone with you at the examination if it is considered helpful.

You have to explain the symptoms of your complaint. Make sure you have a full list of your symptoms. Be exact and do not make yourself seem better than you are. Include any symptoms that might not be present at the time of the medical examination because you suffer from a medical condition that fluctuates in its severity.

The decision of the doctor or doctors is sent to you in writing. Their reasons and findings should be clear and capable of being understood by anyone unfamiliar with medical matters. Your rights of appeal will be explained in the notification sent to you.

You can appeal to a medical appeal tribunal against the decision of a doctor or medical board within 3 months of the decision being sent to you. There is, however, no right of appeal against an initial assessment for the prescribed industrial disease 'occupational deafness'. And there are certain restrictions on the right of appeal where either pneumoconiosis or byssinosis is involved.

the medical appeal tribunal

In preparing an appeal to the medical appeal tribunal, any independent medical evidence you can obtain will be of great importance and should be sent to the clerk to the tribunal before the hearing.

A general practitioner is not allowed to charge for providing a certificate or report in connection with a benefit claim. But a medical specialist can charge for a report – and the fee can be high. If you qualify for legal advice and assistance under the 'green form' scheme, the solicitor may be able to commission such a report for you under the scheme.

You can claim travel expenses to go to the hearing, and can ask the clerk for the payment in advance or a travel warrant. You may have to travel some distance: medical appeal tribunals are held in only about 20 places over the country.

The hearing is usually conducted in a more formal manner than other appeal tribunals.

The Secretary of State is represented by an officer from the regional office of the DHSS. The legally qualified chairman is flanked by two medical members, who may want to examine you and ask a lot of questions. In a claim concerning mobility allowance, they may want to see you walk (unless you are completely unable to walk). The Child Poverty Action Group's *Rights Guide to Non-means-tested Benefits* advises that "you should tell them what you find difficult (e.g. climbing steps). Insist that they see you walking out of doors if you have greater difficulty doing this than walking indoors."

You are notified of the decision in writing. You can appeal to the social security commissioners only on a point of law. You have to obtain leave to do so from the chairman of the medical appeal tribunal within 3 months of the decision being sent to you. If leave to appeal is refused, you can apply for leave to the commissioners within 28 days of the chairman's refusal of leave being sent to you. Once leave is obtained, you have 3 months to lodge the appeal. If you do not apply for leave of the tribunal chairman within 3 months, you may apply direct to the commissioners, who have discretion to extend the period of 3 months if there are special reasons.

attendance allowance

NI leaflet 205 gives details of attendance allowance for disabled people who need a lot of attention or supervision, and includes a claim form.

If you are unhappy with the attendance allowance board's decision on your claim, you can ask for a review of the decision within 3 months of the decision being sent to you. A review entails a fresh examination and decision by different doctors.

Another doctor will visit you in your home. You must tell the doctor the type of supervision and attention you need both by day and at night. You will be asked what you are capable of doing for yourself – getting into bed, turning over in bed, using the stairs, dressing, washing, eating, drinking, going to the lavatory. Note down in advance your ability in performing these tasks. Keep a diary for fluctuating conditions. Let the doctor know what you really can and cannot do. Be honest about your condition but do not minimise the limitations you suffer from.

It is a good idea to have a sensible and level-headed friend with you during the home visit, who can be an extra check on what questions the doctor asked and how you answered. It is easy when nervous to forget what was said or to give the wrong answer.

A decision may also be reviewed at any time if the decision was based on a mistake as to, or ignorance of, a material fact, or if the circumstances have changed.

If you want to apply for two reviews within 12 months, you need leave to apply for the second review, giving reasons why you think that the decision should now be changed.

An unsuccessful application for a review can be appealed to a social security commissioner, but only on a point of law, within 3 months of the unfavourable review decision.

Housing benefit reviews

Housing benefit is administered by local authorities. The review machinery lies within the local authority itself and there is no second tier of appeal to an independent commissioner.

A local authority must decide on a claim for housing benefit within 14 days, or as soon as is reasonably practicable. If the local authority does not decide within 14 days, it must make an interim payment to tenants on supplementary benefit in private sector accommodation and housing association tenants, unless the local authority has not been given any information about the rent payable.

The local authority must inform you of any decision it takes relating to your entitlement to housing benefit and you can ask for an explanation of how your entitlement, or lack of it, has been calculated. This must be given to you within 14 days of your request. A CAB or other advice agency can help you check this and advise you if your entitlement appears to have been calculated incorrectly.

You can ask for a review of the council's decision on your housing benefit, by writing within 6 weeks of the decision. You have to set out the reason why you would like the decision to be re-considered (such as a miscalculation). The review will normally be made by officials in the local authority department responsible for housing benefit. They should then let you know in writing whether the council's original decision is upheld or amended.

If you are not satisfied with this first review, you can appeal to a review board composed of at least three councillors, who should not have been previously involved in the case under review.

You should apply to the board at the local authority housing benefit section, within 28 days of getting the review decision (unless you have good reason for any delay), stating the grounds why you want an appeal. It could be, for example, that the local authority considers the amount you pay in rent and rates excessive and is calculating your housing benefit on less than you actually pay out. There are set criteria as to what the local authority should consider in arriving at this decision and you may be able to challenge the assessment that your rent and rates are excessive.

A hearing must be given within 6 weeks of your application and you must be given reasonable notice of the hearing – normally at least two weeks. You can be represented, or can attend and present your own case and call your witnesses, just as you would at a social security appeal tribunal.

Make sure you read and understand the rules thoroughly before you get anywhere near the review board's hearing. The publication *A guide to housing benefits* (£4.50) available from SHAC (The London Housing Aid Centre), 189a Old Brompton Road, London SW5 0AR, includes a comprehensive section on 'Reviewing decisions' with a helpful flow chart of the sequence of notifications, representations and appeals.

Prepare a written copy of your argument, quoting the relevant regulations, to be given to each councillor. This also helps you to plan the presentation of your case so that you do not miss any points.

The review board may reach a decision at the end of a hearing. If it defers its decision, you should be notified within 7 days of the decision being reached.

Unlike other benefits, there is no further right of appeal from the decision of the review board. The courts may be able to intervene if you apply for judicial review, but you will need a lawyer to help you with this course of action.

ombudsman

Local authorities have to act fairly in carrying out their duties. If there is any undue delay, or bias, or if papers are lost or the local authority has failed to keep you informed, or has done anything that could amount to 'maladministration', you can complain to the local ombudsman (commissioner for complaints, in Northern Ireland).

You cannot complain if you are just unhappy with the decision – for the ombudsman to investigate, there must be something wrong in the procedure that has been followed.

You should approach your local councillor first, and if he cannot solve the problem and refuses to pass the complaint on to the local ombudsman, you can apply direct. A leaflet about the local ombudsman service can be obtained from most citizens advice bureaux.

glossary

affidavit
a statement in writing containing a person's evidence in detail, set out in numbered paragraphs, sworn as true before a solicitor or a court officer

affirming
binding promise to speak the truth, the whole truth and nothing but the truth, without swearing to do so on the bible or other holy book

bench
magistrates (lay or stipendiary) before whom a criminal case is tried

chambers
the registrar's or judge's room; when a case is heard 'in chambers', it is normally held in private, with no members of the public or the press allowed to be present; proceedings tend to be less formal than in open court

civil law
that part of the law which confers rights and imposes duties on individuals and deals with resolving disputes between them

conviction
the formal finding by a court establishing the guilt of a person who has committed a criminal offence

counsel
a barrister

criminal law
that part of the law which punishes behaviour which is harmful to the community as a whole

decree
judgment

default action
when only money is being claimed, no date for hearing is fixed but if defendant does not respond within 14 days, plaintiff can ask the court to enter judgment ordering the money to be paid by defendant

defendant
the person against whom a civil case is brought; in criminal proceedings, the person who is alleged to have committed an offence

directions
registrar's or judge's instructions to plaintiff or defendant about what has to be done before a case can proceed to the next stage

discovery and disclosure
a method of enabling each party to see all the relevant documents in the possession of his opponent, by each first letting the other know what documents exist and then allowing the other party to inspect any of them (except privileged ones). The court can be asked by either party to direct disclosure/discovery by the other

filing
leaving documents (notices, applications, particulars of claim, affidavit etc) with the court office for sealing and service

fixed-date action
when a claim is not solely for a sum of money, the date for hearing is fixed and put on the summons

hearsay evidence
indirect knowledge of an event, not seen or heard or experienced by the person giving evidence, but told to him by somebody else; not allowed in open court (but less strictly disallowed by registrar in chambers)

indictable offence
an offence which is triable at the crown court with judge and jury; the procedure starts with committal in the magistrates' court

judgment
formal decision of the court; it normally includes an order that one party pay to the other a specified sum or that one party give possession of property or return goods to the other. The expression covers both the written document containing details of the court's decision and the oral statement of the judge or registrar at the conclusion of a case. When a plaintiff applies for judgment to be given in default of a defence, this is referred to as 'entering judgment'

leading question
question which suggests the answer the questioner wants/expects to get; not allowed when examining own witness, but all right when cross-examining witness of opponent

liquidated damages
where the precise sum claimed is known at the outset – as opposed to unliquidated damages where the amount of the damages has to be decided by the court

lodging
another word for filing

mitigation
a person taking civil proceedings is under a duty to 'mitigate his loss' – that is, to take reasonable steps to keep the loss as low as possible
a 'plea in mitigation' is put to the court by a person convicted of an offence before the court decides on the penalty, setting out reasons why the fine or other punishment should be less severe than it would otherwise be

nisi
an interim order which has to be made absolute before it comes fully into effect (literally 'unless')

notice of application
a document giving details of what order is being sought from the court; a copy is sent to the opposing party who can respond before the hearing or attend and make representations when the court hears the application and decides whether to make the order that is requested

offence
a breach of the criminal law

originating application
the notice of application which starts a case; used instead of 'particulars of claim' in certain types of claim

particulars of claim
the document in which the plaintiff sets out the facts on which his claim against the defendant is based and states what judgment or order he is seeking

plaintiff
the person bringing a civil case

plaint note
receipt for court fee for issue of summons; gives the official number of the case

privileged
any document or letter that can be kept from the knowledge of the court and one's opponent (as against matters or documents that have to be disclosed)

respondent
the defendant in a civil case in the magistrates' court; also the 'defendant' in certain civil proceedings started by originating summons or originating application in the High Court or county court

sealing
when the court office puts an official stamp on a document

service
the method by which documents (applications, affidavits, summons etc) are supplied to the parties by or on behalf of the person issuing them or by the court

set aside
making a court order inoperative because it was improperly issued

sheriff (Scotland)
law officer before whom a criminal case is tried, with or without a jury

subpoena
when the court orders a witness or an expert to attend a hearing to give evidence; a witness summons

summons
document issued by the court instructing a person to do something, generally to attend court as defendant or witness

writ
the document with which proceedings in the High Court are started (equivalent to a summons plus particulars of claim in the county court)

index

CA publications include

Approaching retirement
Divorce: legal procedures and financial facts
Earning money at home
A handbook of consumer law
Householder's action guide
The legal side of buying a house (England and Wales)
Living with stress
Renting and letting
Starting your own business
What to do when someone dies
What will my pension be?
The *Which?* book of insurance
The *Which?* book of money
Which? way to buy, sell and move house
Which? way to complain
Wills and probate (England and Wales)

CA publications are available from Consumers' Association, Castlemead, Gascoyne Way, Hertford SG14 1LH and from booksellers